Behind the Blue Lights

by

Mark E. Nickerson

D0062173

North Country Press

Behind the Blue Lights

ISBN 978-1-943424-07-8
Library of Congress Catalog Number 2015951746

Edited by Beth Staples

An adaptation of this photo was used for the cover: (http://billionphotos.com/Media/Detail/716339) by Viernest / CC BY 3.0 (http://creativecommons.org/licenses/by/3.0/)

North Country Press
Unity, Maine

Dedication

It wasn't hard for me to decide whom to dedicate this book to. April 9, 1994, my life changed forever with the arrival of my son, Maxim Evan Nickerson.

Everyone told me how it would change my life and I didn't believe them. I kept telling myself that it would be no big deal and that life would go on as I knew it. I couldn't imagine why or how it would change.

Was I ever wrong. It was instantaneous for me. He was put in my arms the moment he was born and my life changed forever. Instant unconditional love.

I have never been more proud of anyone in my life. To top it all off, he is a good man. He is very active in his church and has gone on numerous church mission trips to Guatemala— always helping out.

He wanted to join the military at the earliest possible time and his mother and I signed the papers for him to do that.

I can't say a bad word about my son, even when he torments me for the fun of it.

One of my funniest moments with Max was when he was 3 or 4 years old. I was still an active trooper and we all know the jokes about cops and doughnuts! I was driving through Winslow one day and a new Dunkin' Donuts was being built. My little boy, cute as ever, saw the doughnut shop, pointed at it and said, "Look Daddy, they're building you a new office!"

So you can see he's a character as well. Whatever he chooses for his career path, I will be 100 percent behind him. And who knows, one day there may be another Nickerson with the Maine State Police force.

Foreword

When Mark Nickerson asked me to write the foreword for this book I was honored. Mark graciously included a few of our adventures together in his last book, and I even won the superlative of being the "worst" driver he had ever ridden with, a superlative that I don't necessarily agree with, but nonetheless am pleased to be the "best-worst" driver he has ever seen!

When I first met Mark I was a young trooper working in some of the most beautiful parts of this great state of Maine. Mark was an even younger rookie, and was all "spit and polish." Early in his career I was assigned as Mark's FTO (Field Training Officer).

There is a very humorous story about Mark's first experience with a drunk driver in his first book, "Blue Lights in the Night." While it is humorous now, at the time it ended with Mark getting quite the stern lecture from me. The broom beating I received at the time from dear ol' Judy didn't help in me being particularly understanding of the situation either.

This drunk driver arrest was the first of many for Trooper Nickerson. He had a remarkable knack for spotting drivers under the influence and during his career he successfully apprehended more than 1,000 drunk drivers, an accolade that earned him a trip to the White House to be honored by President Bill Clinton.

One story that Mark did not include in his book is one that still to this day gives me a chuckle, and probably after all this time Mark can now laugh about it as well. One afternoon both Mark and I were dispatched to an accident. While I was en route to the scene from patrolling in another location, Mark was responding from home. Hopping in his cruiser, he began reversing out of his garage. Just at this time, I contacted him on the radio to get his whereabouts. As he keyed his mic to respond, it activated his automatic garage door and, unbeknownst to him, closed the door. As Mark was explaining that he was en route himself, I heard an awful crunch, and then a few choice words from Trooper Nickerson. The garage door had taken his light bar clean off his cruiser…and he calls me the worst driver he has ever seen!

In all seriousness, it truly was an honor to work with Mark. I knew that he would turn into a great trooper and I would like to think that I might have bestowed some wisdom upon him during our days together. But the truth is Mark was born to be an officer. The Maine State Police is a brotherhood of sorts, just as other law enforcement and public safety departments are. I am honored to call Mark my "brother," just as anyone who had the pleasure of working with and getting to know him is.

Paul T. Davis
State Senator, District 4
Retired Maine State Police

Introduction

I have to admit, this writing thing has opened up a whole new experience in my life. I never would have thought how much fun reliving my career and sharing it with the public could be.

Retired Warden John Ford (author of three books) and I have gone all over the state of Maine and New Hampshire telling stories about our careers. Nothing makes us happier than hearing people laugh and enjoy an evening out of the house. Our goal is to always leave them laughing and most of the time I think we succeed.

It didn't start out too easy, though. At my first three talks, I encountered people I had arrested for drunk driving. When I was first approached by these people and they admitted what they had done, I wasn't sure how it was going to go.

I quickly was put at ease when Bob met me in Rangeley. "You arrested me for OUI 33 years ago! One of the funniest nights of my life! Can I have my picture taken with you?"

Of course, I obliged and we went over the details of his arrest all those years ago and had a big laugh all over again. He now counsels for his career.

The next one was in Belfast. The lady who arranged the talk asked me if I remembered her. I didn't. "Well you arrested me for OUI when I was still a teenager. You opened my eyes. I had no idea that I was doing something so wrong."

Then, of course, there was the time in Freedom when I was telling a story about a drunk driver who John and I picked up one very cold winter night. After telling the story, a gentleman came up to me afterward and said, "You know that story you told about the OUI you got one cold night?"

"Yes," I replied.

"That's my boy. Never was too bright."

Some of the people we run into tell us some of the funniest incidents that occurred in their life as well. I thought I would share at least a couple with you that I still laugh at whenever I think of them.

One night in Augusta we were invited to have supper at the historical society before the talk. So Johnny and I were lunching with a whole bunch of people at the Friendly's restaurant.

One of the ladies was quite intrigued with our stories and she finally told us that she had one that she thought might be funny as well.

She told us about when she was in her early 20s and was married to a doctor. He had this very temperamental foreign sports car that he liked to take to work at the hospital.

As the weather got colder in the fall, the car sometimes would not start.

One morning, as cold as it was, sure enough the car would not start. Her husband went back into the house and woke this lady and told her he needed assistance. So she got up, put on a robe, and went out to help him.

Her husband described to her that he needed a push to jump start the car. His instructions were that he had to get going 25 mph while she pushed him down the road. Then he could jump it and be off.

So the lady got in their regular car, went down the street, turned around and got going 25 mph. Then she crashed into the back of the sports car, wrecking both cars. She told us they got divorced not long after that little incident.

Just recently, John and I were in Palermo giving a talk and afterward a lady asked if I knew her dad, who used to be a Waterville cop. I did, in fact, know him and had interacted with him several times over the years.

She then told me one of the funniest stories that she ever heard from him.

On patrol one evening, her dad was training a rookie officer. The rookie was a big boy and always seemed to be munching or looking for something to eat.

They got a call to do a welfare check on an elderly lady that the family had not heard from for a few days. They went to the address and found a way into the home when no one answered the door. Once inside, they found the lady in her living room chair, with the TV on and her knitting in her lap. She was deceased.

The necessary calls were made to other officials and the family.

The rookie noticed a bowl of peanuts on the stand beside the chair where the deceased was sitting.

The rookie helped himself to the peanuts by the handful. The veteran cop kept telling him not to eat them. This was a scene and not to be disturbed.

The rookie argued that she was gone, it wouldn't matter to her. And he kept munching on the peanuts.

Finally one of the lady's relatives came to identify her.

The relative said, "Oh look, how peaceful she died, doing what she loves. Sitting in her favorite chair, watching TV, knitting and eating chocolate-covered peanuts."

The veteran officer said, "Chocolate-covered peanuts?"

"Oh yes, she takes her teeth out, and puts the chocolate covered peanuts in her mouth to melt the chocolate off and then puts the peanuts in a bowl on the stand beside the chair."

I have to admit, I never saw that one coming.

The remarks we get at most of our talks are priceless. You can read a few of them at www.oldcops.com.

One of the remarks that got me laughing was said at a well-attended talk in Pittsfield. There were close to 150 people or so there; it was an awards night with a dinner and drinks.

John and I were the entertainment for the evening. After the talk while we were selling our books, a very lovely lady told us how she rode to the event with several other people. They discussed who the entertainment was that evening and learned that it was an old trooper and an even older game warden who would be speaking.

This lady told us, "Now what in the world could these guys be talking about to us! I thought we were going to be getting a safety talk of some kind. I just want you to know our table was taken by complete surprise and we haven't been that entertained for years! You did a great job."

Both John and I got a big kick out of her comments and also were very appreciative of them.

One of the most heart-wrenching encounters occurred one day in Augusta. John and I were to do a book-signing at Barnes & Noble. Usually John and I travel together but on this day we couldn't. I arrived about 5 minutes before we were supposed to start. John was early as usual and the crowd was quite large.

As I entered, John had some wise remark for me, "Hey Nummy, you got people waiting for you! Hurry up and get over here."

I strolled over to the table set up for us and a family approached. The mom, (I assumed) hugged me, hanging on for quite some time.

The other people gathered around me. I had no idea who they were but kept hugging the mom.

I noticed there were tears and it started to get kind of emotional. Then a gentleman said, "We are the Dostie family. Parents and family of Sgt. Tom Dostie."

It hit me like a sledge hammer. I had all I could do to hold back the tears. They were there to thank me for including a story about their son in my first book.

I had been fortunate to be able to escort his body from the Portland Jetport to a funeral home in Windsor, Maine.

I was completely speechless as they spoke to me. I couldn't have talked if I wanted to anyway.

After they left it took a good half-hour for me to settle down and do the business at hand. John kept asking me what that was all about and all I could say was, "I'll tell you later."

So here are a bunch more stories from my career and a couple from the archives that I thought you might enjoy. I also have included a couple stories from other officers. Believe me, any police officer who worked the road has a book in them if they want to share their experiences.

I tell it like it was for me and to repeat it again, you just can't make this stuff up! Hope you enjoy.

Mark E. Nickerson
September 2015

Table of Contents

All in the Family

My middle brother has a beautiful year-round camp on Three Mile Pond in Vassalboro. It has two stories with balconies overlooking a great room.

The great room is grand indeed. It has cathedral ceilings and a stone fireplace covers one whole wall. An all-glass wall faces the lake and four huge columns enclose the porch area. It once was a beautiful older camp owned by a doctor. The grounds were meticulously kept as well.

One winter day, my brother called and said he thought his camp had been broken into. He had received the monthly phone bill and noticed that someone had made calls in the middle of the night from the camp.

A few days before getting the phone bill, he had checked on the lakeside retreat and noticed an open window. When he went inside to close the window he noticed that snow had blown in and the heating pipes had frozen. He thought the wind had blown open the window and he remedied the situation.

However, since getting the phone bill, he thought someone had entered the camp and, at the very least, used the phone.

My brother asked me to look into this and to see to whom the calls had been made. He gave me the phone bill and I simply called the numbers.

I noticed all the calls were to the Augusta area. When I dialed the first number a gentleman answered the phone.

"Yes, sir, this is Trooper Nickerson with the Maine State Police. I'm investigating a burglary that took place in a camp in the Vassalboro area on the 17th of this month. The reason I'm calling you is that your phone number was called from the camp on that date around midnight. Could I please have your name?"

"Yes, this is Mr. Smith."

"Do you remember getting any phone calls on that date at that time, sir?"

"Well, no, I don't. But hang on a minute and let me check with my son."

I waited a few seconds and Mr. Smith came back on the phone. "Trooper Nickerson?"

"Yes."

"I checked with my son and he said he was the one who got the call that night."

"And what is your son's name?"

"Simon."

At that moment, I knew the investigation was over.

My brother's son, Jimmy, was a Cony High School basketball player. The boys on the squad had played together for most of their school years. I had followed Jimmy's career and watched as many games as I could. And I knew all the other players' names as well. As soon as he said 'Simon,' I knew exactly with whom I was speaking.

"Simon the basketball player from Cony?"

"Yes. And he said that Jimmy Nickerson called him that night at that time," said Mr. Smith.

"Uh-huh," was about all I could muster.

"Is this still an official investigation," Mr. Smith asked.

"Nope, not anymore! I'm sorry to have bothered you, and I thank you for your information," I said and hung up the phone.

The next phone call went to my dear brother.

"Mike, do you want to know who broke into your camp?"

"Of course," he said.

"It was your son."

"Oh really! Why that little *%$^*&@! I'll take care of him. Thanks for letting me know."

I never did find out what was said between them but I did learn that Jimmy had a key to the camp after that so he wouldn't have to go through any more open windows.

A Keen Eye

While still pretty new with the Maine State Police, I had to travel from Greenville to Bangor one day for a criminal case.

While en route to Bangor, I asked my field training officer, Cpl. Paul Davis, if he wanted to ride with me to assist with the interview. Paul said sure and, after picking him up in Sangerville, off we went to Bangor.

We arrived in the big city and while traveling through some of the side streets, we came to a stop sign at a T-intersection. I have an interest in autos, and the unusual ones always catch my eye.

While parked at the stop sign in the intersection, I noticed two identical Volkswagens parked in the driveway across the street. They were both VW bugs and were even the same color. Parked side by side, I kept noticing something wasn't right and after staring long enough, I realized that both VWs had the same license plate number. I kind of chuckled about this to myself, then mentioned it to Paul. He caught on right away and said to me, in only his way, "That's pretty observant, young fella!"

Still being pretty new, this was a nice compliment from someone who didn't give many. Of course, we discussed it further and decided nothing could be done about it as the vehicles were parked off the public way.

However, I did tip off the Bangor Police Department of the situation and asked them to keep an eye out for the vehicles. I certainly appreciated Paul's comment and I also thought I was being quite observant to notice that someone was trying to save money by not registering one of their cars.

Fast-forward about 10 years. That funny old game warden John Ford rode with me for about eight years nonstop. One night working the Waldo County area, the warden from Brooks was riding with me as usual. We were in the Palermo area, just off Route 3 near a monument. I had a driver stopped for a minor traffic violation, and was talking with the operator in my cruiser.

John was in the backseat half paying attention, probably looking for something to amuse himself with while I conducted my business in the front. There wasn't much traffic going by, as it was quite late at night on a back road. I figured John would doze off shortly.

While talking with the operator, two vehicles passed by that seemed to be together. I wasn't paying attention, as I was dealing with the violator.

All of a sudden, John came to life in the backseat and said, "You know, I think those two vehicles that just went by had the same license plate on them."

As much as I hate to admit it, John was right more than he was wrong, so I asked him if it was worth a look. John said, "Yep." I booted the violator out after issuing him paperwork and took off after the two suspect vehicles.

John and I came up behind the vehicles traveling north on the North Palermo Road. After observing the vehicles for a bit, it became evident they did have matching license plate numbers. So they were definitely going to get stopped.

It gets pretty tricky trying to stop two vehicles at once, so I waited for the right road condition and location. When the time was right, I made my move to pursue and stop the lead vehicle, then jumped out to flag the second vehicle over before it got by us.

The stop was successful, and both John and I got out to approach the operators. Turns out they were John's neighbors from Jackson. They were brothers from a nice, hard-working family. They questioned why they were being pulled over, and John and I had the biggest smiles on our faces as we joked with them and asked, "You mean you don't know why?"

They both played dumb for a while, then I thought I'd mention the license plates to them. Talk about getting caught with your hand in the cookie jar! They were truly shocked that we figured out what they were up to and they could not believe that we noticed the license plates on the vehicles.

They told us they had gone to Massachusetts that day to look at a vehicle and ended up buying it. The only way to get it home was to put a plate on it from the vehicle they went to Massachusetts in. They were laughing as they passed so many police officers on the way home and didn't get caught. After they got through Augusta, they figured they had it made, as it was mostly back roads the rest of the way.

They were just miles from home when they got caught. We all had a good laugh and I got writer's cramps issuing them summonses to visit the judge at District Court in Belfast.

I hated to give John a compliment, but I couldn't help it. He truly had been observant and noticed the little things. I told him about the time I noticed the same thing in Bangor, but those cars were stopped. Ol' John Boy was able to do it while the vehicles were going down the road and in the dark.

Good job, Johnny! Too bad they were your neighbors.

A Long Hot Ride

Whenever we get those really hot, humid, hazy, sweaty days in the summer time, I'm reminded of a particular case in the early '80s when I had to lug a couple of criminals from Winslow to the Waldo County Jail in Belfast—pre-air conditioning days for cruisers.

This story involves a couple of guys who were constant thorns in the side of law enforcement in Waldo and Kennebec counties. I first came across this group of thugs when they were caught harboring a fugitive from the Maine State Prison. Seems a prisoner was out on furlough and just never bothered to return to the prison. Well, he was caught in downtown Unity one afternoon — hence my introduction to this outlaw group. After the capture of the prisoner, the case was investigated further, and this group was found to have been hiding the prisoner for many days.

One of the guys in this group just loved to antagonize my buddy, John Ford, the local game warden. Seems like every time Curly saw John he sucked in on his cigarette and while puffing out, drawled in only the way he could, "Good day to kill a deer, huh John?"

Curly had a raspy voice that went right through you. Even though John would not let on to Curly that it bothered him, I knew that it was eating up John. But as we say in the cop world, "It's a long road without a curve!"

And all we had to do was just keep on this group. We knew they would get caught at something sooner or later. Just about all the men in this group were heavy drinkers, were involved in drugs, were violent when they needed to be and tried to intimidate anyone who got in their way.

I tried to make sure they saw me at least once a day, and most times it was not a pleasant greeting that I got in return. Over the course of several months, many cases were worked and finally enough evidence was gathered to make an arrest.

We looked and looked for our "friends," but for some reason they were laying low and could not be located. We seemed to be just missing them every time we looked for them, or they were staying very well hidden.

Then one very hot humid summer day, my warden friend Ford was riding with me and we were leaving the Waterville/Winslow area, heading east in my 1982 Chevrolet Malibu State Police cruiser.

Let me tell you about this so-called cruiser. This was the first time ever the state police had purchased a mid-sized car for a cruiser. It was way too small, had no air-conditioning and, to make things worse, the rear windows would not roll down. Therefore, you could not get much air into the cruiser. It was hot all the time.

This was also the first year of bucket seats. They were a terrible seat, too small and gave no support for a good-sized man. Seems like I was shoulder to shoulder with anyone who rode with me in the front of that vehicle. It was extremely uncomfortable.

To make matters worse, no matter how hard I tried to destroy this vehicle, it would not die. I ended up driving it for almost two years before there were enough miles on it to send it to the auction. In short, this was clearly the worst cruiser I drove my entire career.

So we were headed east on Route 137 out of Winslow when we spotted a vehicle driving west on the same road. This vehicle was very familiar as it was used by our group of thugs. As we met the vehicle, both John and I recognized the two occupants as being wanted.

Neither of them had a driver's license, and their right to operate were suspended anyway. It also was a good chance the driver would be under the influence of something. I flipped around and pursued the suspect vehicle.

Surprisingly, the suspect vehicle pulled over and stopped. Curly was driving, but the other thug was the one to watch. He was one I wanted to keep in front of me at all times. I didn't trust anything he did. He was, in my opinion, a very dangerous person. (This proved to be true in the not-too-distant future.)

Both John and I approached the vehicle, me to the driver side and John to the passenger side. They were quickly arrested and handcuffed and we started to bring them back to the cruiser.

As I escorted Curly back to the cruiser, I got him to the rear of his vehicle before he spotted John. Curly is about 6 feet tall, weighs about 350 pounds, always leaves his shirt completely unbuttoned and smells like he has never showered.

As a matter of fact, every time I was at his residence, chickens and goats wandered through the house most of the time. To say the least, he stunk, and stunk very bad.

But as Curly saw John, Curly just could not resist egging John on and said, "Good day to kill a deer, huh John?"

Well, when Curly turned to throw that insult, he lost his balance, tripped, fell and rolled right down the embankment, coming to rest at the bottom of the ditch. It was probably 6-7 feet below the road. Old Curly was wallowing around and just cussing up a storm.

In response to Curly, John said "Good day to go to jail, huh Curly?"

I finally climbed down and helped Curly out of the ditch and into the back of the cruiser to be seated with his friend.

The warrants were out of Belfast, so we had to take these guys there, a 45-mile trip. Did I mention it was hot? And that this car had no cool air coming in?

Needless to say, putting those two guys into that cruiser was like putting a garbage truck loaded with old, dead, rotten fish in my cruiser. It took me close to an hour to get to Belfast and that was one of the longest, hottest, smelliest rides of my life.

Just another day.

The Rich and Famous

One day in August 2002, I got a phone call about providing protection for a U.S. senator who was going to visit and campaign for a local candidate.

I was advised the senator was Joe Lieberman from Connecticut and that he was going to campaign along the Midcoast for Chellie Pingree, who was running against Susan Collins for the U.S. Senate seat.

I had heard Lieberman many times before on the "Imus in The Morning" radio show, and enjoyed listening to him banter with Imus. He spoke very well, and most of the time I liked what I heard from him. Lieberman also had been Al Gore's running mate in the 2000 presidential race.

Even though the Gore-Lieberman ticket did not win, I thought Lieberman was clearly a man of honor and a true gentleman. I thought it would be a nice change of pace to spend an afternoon with someone of such historical importance.

I was to meet the plane at the Owls Head airport, catch up with the senator's security people and map out the day with them regarding where to go and the best routes to travel. Lieberman's security was provided by the United States Capitol Police. I learned of his itinerary upon my arrival, and we started to make plans for the day.

The first stop was at Don McLean's house in Camden. At first, this name didn't ring any bells with me. I have listened to the song "American Pie" since the 1970s when it first came out, and I have heard it on the radio ever since. It's one of those songs I never tire of hearing.

The songwriter and performer is, of course, Don McLean. However, I did not make the connection as I did not know he lived in Maine. And not only in Maine, but right in Camden.

I kept looking at the Capitol Police as though to ask, "Are you sure he lives in Maine?" All these years, and I never knew such a celebrity lived right here.

I had wanted the detail for the historical aspect of protecting a U.S. senator and former vice presidential candidate, but the detail kept getting better and better, in that I also would get to visit a truly classic performer.

While waiting for the senator to arrive, we arranged the motorcade and engaged in small talk. I had, of course, brought my camera. I asked security if I could get a picture with Lieberman, if there was any time and it would not inconvenience anyone.

The security force said they would check and, if time allowed, take care of that for me so that I would have a memento of the occasion.

Finally, the plane carrying the senator arrived and — after greeting all the local candidates — Lieberman and Pingree were escorted from the airport to our first destination, McLean's home.

Myself with Sen. Joe Leiberman at Owls Head Airport.

We arrived and got all the people where they needed to be. This was a fundraiser for Pingree and there were a lot of rich people attending. It was quite elaborate with music, food, speeches and lots of entertainment. After making sure people were where they wanted to be, it was our time to take in the whole scene.

The home was absolutely gorgeous, nestled high in the mountains, with views of both the ocean and lakes. The grounds were manicured and immaculate. To put it simply, it was breathtaking. I was still pinching myself that we were at the McLean house. Who knew!

After a few hours at the party, we whisked Lieberman to another stop before getting him back to the airport.

While waiting for him at the second stop, I was advised that the senator would be happy to have a photo taken with me. This, of course, brought a big smile to my face.

After leaving the second stop, however, the people riding with me had to make a slight detour, and I did not make it back to the airport at the same time as Lieberman. I was a good five minutes away when they asked my estimated time of arrival at the airport. I advised them, "Thanks, but don't wait up for me," as I did not want to hold him up, especially just for a photograph.

I arrived at the airport and to my surprise, the plane carrying Lieberman was still there and the senator was outside talking with his aides. One of the Capitol Police officers said Lieberman was waiting for me to get a photo.

I was so flustered that I was holding everyone up, I just tried to tell them not to worry about it, that they must be in a hurry. Again the Capitol Police officer told me to get over with the senator, as he was waiting for me. I grabbed my camera, got out of my cruiser and approached him.

I quickly learned why Lieberman is a well-known, important and successful politician. He immediately made me feel like a friend. He greeted me by my first name. Then, he asked about my last name, stating he knew some Nickersons in Connecticut. Fortunately, I had just studied my ancestry and was able to relate to him something that was at least informative. He was such an easy person to speak with.

The senator had me give my camera to one of his aides and several photos were taken. I thanked him for his time and apologized to him for holding him up, to which he replied, "It was my pleasure."

Lieberman boarded his plane with his entourage and taxied onto the runway for takeoff. While watching the plane soar into the blue sky, I thought to myself, "What a job I have!"

What made this day even more special was a personal one. At the time of this detail, my son Max was 8 years old. Soon after, Max heard the song "American Pie." He was intrigued and the more he heard it, the more he liked it, and the more he asked me about it.

I told him about the time I was at the singer's house in Maine. My son did not believe me, so I brought out the photos of myself and Lieberman, and the photos I took of Don McLean's home.

Max was in awe. This song became one of his favorites and he played it frequently, especially while showering. If we came home and heard that song blaring, we knew Max was in the shower!

A couple of years after this detail, Don McLean performed at the Lobster Festival in Rockland. You can only imagine that I took my son to watch him. What a grand time we had, especially when he sang "American Pie."

Just another day.

Brotherhood is Strong

In the summer of 2006 I had the pleasure of volunteering to work at camps in the Jackman area that are paid for by the Maine State Troopers Foundation. One of the foundation's purposes is to serve underprivileged children.

When I worked there, I met New Jersey State Trooper James Kiernan, who patrolled in the upper portion of that state. I told him that I wanted to see Ground Zero in New York City. Ever since 9/11 it had been in the back of my mind to visit Ground Zero. It was important to me because on no other day in the history of America has this country lost so many police officers and firefighters. I had to go there, see it for myself and pay my respects to the police officers and all others who lost their lives that day.

I asked how difficult it was to drive into the city. He started to tell me that it was quite easy, and before he got around to giving directions, he said, "Let me give you my card. When you know you are coming, give me a day's notice and I will arrange for you to go on patrol with our marine division and they can take you there."

Ground Zero where the Twin Towers used to be.

To say the least I was flabbergasted. I asked, "Are you sure?" He said he was. I warned him that I was definitely going to be contacting him and taking advantage of the offer.

Later in the year, I had just that opportunity while traveling through New York. As planned, I contacted Trooper Keirnan and within the hour he called back and said it was all arranged and told me where to go and whom to meet.

You can believe I had him tell me over and over the exact directions on how to get to the Trooper Barrack in Port Newark. I have to admit that I get rather nervous driving in a big city when I'm not familiar with where I am going. I left early in the morning in case I got lost. A great decision as I did, in fact, get lost.

Do you know what it's like to look for turns as traffic piles up behind you, with motorists honking horns and making gestures? And when I missed a turn or made a wrong one, it took quite a while to get going in the right direction. But finally I made it to my destination at the Port. And I sighed a huge sigh of relief.

As soon as I introduced myself, I was treated like one of the family. From the lieutenant on down, I was offered all the benefits this location had to offer.

It was arranged that I would go on patrol with three troopers, Sgt. Todd Schmidt, Cpl. Ken Pilanski and Trooper Ed Schnezler on a 44-foot patrol boat. The boat was powered by two 671-horsepower diesel engines and could travel at a speed of about 30 knots. Pretty fast for such a big boat. This was one of many boats in the fleet. The boats are named in honor of New Jersey troopers killed in the line of duty.

Myself, right, and three NJ state troopers on their 44-foot patrol boat.

I was given a rundown of what was to happen, what I should do and what their duties were. After the briefing, off we went into the bay. The day was sunny and gorgeous and it was great to be on the water. The New Jersey troopers' main responsibility is to patrol the northern shore of the state, checking ports, boats, bridges and whatever else they come across.

I can't tell you what a little corner of the world we live in here in Maine. There is so much going on in other locations of our country, and they are amazing to see and experience. The commerce, ships and activity on the Hudson River were astonishing. We were constantly looking at the goings-on.

We went up into the river by the Statue of Liberty and Ellis Island, under all the bridges and along the shore of lower Manhattan.

I was taken to a port where the *USS Intrepid* was docked. This ship is now a museum, however just recently it was shut down as it's going to be taken out of the water for a restoration. Still, it was an amazing sight.

We stopped for lunch at an old train station on the north shore, then headed off again on patrol. We came down along the shore of lower Manhattan, enjoying the skyline of the busiest city of the world. All the famous landmarks of New York City were pointed out to me as I took picture after picture. The Empire State building, the Chrysler building, Rockefeller Center and on and on.

Finally, we came to a small marina and entered through the break wall. We parked alongside a multi-million dollar yacht and tied off. Sgt Schmidt took me for a walk through a street and into an observatory, and there it was — Ground Zero.

Sgt. Schmidt explained what this place looked like on 9/11, how the New Jersey State Police assisted in evacuating people with the boat, and what it looked like in the months following the terrorist attack.

He said paper from the World Trade Center hung in trees for weeks and the debris pile was stories high. Damage to buildings adjacent to the World Trade Center was enormous.

A marina where debris fell on the NJSP boat while officers
evacuated people from Ground Zero.

Now it's all cleaned up and it was difficult to imagine just
how majestic this place was before it all happened. We only had
a few minutes as Sgt. Schmidt had to get back to work. I
snapped some photos and we left. It was a sight to behold.

I can't thank these troopers enough for giving me the
opportunity to "ride" along with them. The courtesy they
extended to me was most gracious. It makes me feel very
special knowing that I belong to one of the strongest
brotherhoods in this nation — "state troopers."

One more thing before finishing this story. I needed to get
back on the right road to get out of Port Newark and I asked for
very good directions. Sensing my concern, Cpl. Pilanski said he
would escort me to I-78 so I would not get lost. I could not thank
him enough for that extra courtesy.

Stabbing the Dashboard

I used to have a rider along with me quite often on weekends. His name was Ben Pinkham and he was a part-time Somerset County deputy sheriff who helped out in the Rockwood area of Moosehead Lake.

His full-time job was as a registered Maine bear guide. He had camps and many hunters came from all over the country to hunt with him.

To describe Ben is quite easy. The only difficulty was being able to tell the difference between him and the bears that he hunted. Ben was big, burly, hairy and growled a lot.

But under all the gruffness he was a man with a great sense of humor. We had a lot of fun when we rode together, and we earned quite a reputation as a twosome.

This story is just one of the many we experienced together.

It was a snowy night in Piscataquis County. Actually, it was just short of being a major blizzard. I had picked up Ben in Rockwood and headed south on Route 15 toward Guilford.

There was a favorite restaurant/bar in Abbott that provided me with a lot of entertainment over the years, and that night was no exception.

After I picked up Ben, the snow started. Throughout the night it kept getting worse. By the time I made it to Abbott, it was a full-blown storm and the driving was horrendous. I could barely see beyond the hood of my cruiser. I knew that getting Ben back to Rockwood through the North Woods was going to be a long drive later that night.

I remember telling Ben that it looked like it was going to be a quiet night as there seemed to be no traffic whatsoever on the road. Seemed like people were taking the storm seriously and staying at home.

I thought I would make it to Guilford, the southern end of my patrol area, and begin the long drive back north. I was expecting no one at my favorite restaurant/bar but decided to check to see if it had any business.

I was rather surprised to see about a dozen vehicles there. I continued to Guilford, checked around the town, then drove north again. I again told Ben it looked like we weren't going to be stopping many vehicles as we still had not seen any traffic on the road.

We were heading north and were about a half-mile south of the restaurant/bar when all of a sudden, out of the hard-driving snow emerged a vehicle coming right at me.

I did the old pucker-factor thing, swerved hard to the right to avoid a head-on collision and after the vehicle sailed by me, I brought the cruiser back onto the highway, all the while sliding sideways and turning to go after the suspect vehicle.

Ben, for once, was speechless except to say, "Let's get 'em!"

I pursued the vehicle, slipping and sliding every which way, and got it stopped as we came into Guilford. The vehicle was a brand-spanking new Jeep Wagoneer and it had Massachusetts plates on it.

At the time, that was probably one of the best all-wheel-drive vehicles on the market and it was expensive. I approached the operator and Ben kept an eye on the passenger side of the vehicle.

After speaking with the operator and making routine observations, it was clear he was drunk. He explained that he and his friend had come to Maine for the weekend to enjoy some ice-fishing and snowmobiling in the North Maine woods. I told him that was all fine but that drinking then driving was not. I checked on his passenger, who was sitting in the right front seat. He was as drunk, if not more drunk, than the operator.

Due to the situation, I had no choice but to lug the out-of-state operator to jail. My other decision was what to do with his vehicle. That was one reason I had Ben along with me. He usually drove the drunk drivers' vehicles home so a tow truck didn't have to be called.

If you ever want a good laugh, listen to Ben recite all the types of vehicles he drove home. I explained to the drunk operator that I would either have to call a tow truck or he could allow the part-time deputy to drive his vehicle to the hotel in Dover-Foxcroft.

The drunk driver, who was very cooperative, asked if we would drive his Jeep to the hotel. Ben agreed and, after processing the drunk driver, we started for Dover.

No sooner had Ben gotten into the Jeep and started driving, when the brakes came on and Ben stopped. I walked up to see if there was a problem.

Ben told me the drunk passenger was being a little bit unruly. He seemed to be an ugly drunk and did not like that his friend had been arrested for OUI.

I sternly explained to Ben's passenger what had happened and what was going to happen. And I told him if he did not like it, then he could get out and walk to wherever he needed to be. He decided to stay in the vehicle, be good and ride to the hotel with Ben.

We again started for Dover. We got a couple of miles down the road and all of a sudden, the brakes came on hard, and the Jeep swerved hard to the right and stopped by the side of the road.

Before the vehicle had stopped, the driver's door flew open and out came big Ben. He backed away from the vehicle and pointed for me to get up there quickly and help him. I could not imagine what the problem was. Ben was screeching, "This guy's crazy!"

"What did he do?" I asked.

"Look!" screamed Ben.

I looked inside the vehicle and there, stuck right in the middle of the steel dashboard, was a beautiful hunting knife. Ben told me his passenger had pulled the knife out of a sheath, drew back and drove it into the dashboard. The passenger said he was going to do the same thing to Ben.

Ben told me he could not get the vehicle stopped fast enough.

Enough was enough. I called a tow truck and had the brand-new Jeep hauled off. That was right after we dragged the passenger out of the Jeep, handcuffed him and loaded him into the back seat of the cruiser.

I got myself a two-fer — that is, two arrests out of one vehicle. It was comical listening to the arrested OUI driver in my cruiser, asking in disbelief, "He did what to my brand-new Jeep? He stabbed my dashboard? You're kidding, right?"

Just another routine drunk driver on a quiet, snowy night!

The Alarm

One of my favorite subjects to talk about is a certain cruiser I had for a couple of years. In December 1995, I was lucky enough to have a brand-new, bright red 1996 Camaro LT-1 police package cruiser assigned to me.

Just about every day that I drove this vehicle, I had to pinch myself to make sure I wasn't dreaming.

It certainly was an attention-getter and a huge PR tool for the Maine State Police, as it was fully marked and had blue lights on the roof. No matter where I stopped, it drew a crowd of onlookers and curious people.

One afternoon I was driving down Main Street in Waterville, simply minding my own business. An older Toyota sports car buzzed around me, followed me, pulled up alongside me and cut in front of me as the driver constantly checked out my cruiser.

I felt like a queen bee with all the worker bees buzzing around. After he checked out the wheels, he gave me a disgusted look and sped off very quickly. I followed him and clocked him speeding at least 20 miles per hour over the posted speed limit. So I stopped him for that violation. When I approached the operator he said, "That is *not* a real cruiser!"

I got his license, registration and insurance card and told him I would be right back. When I returned, I told him that I was a real police officer, the cruiser was a real police cruiser, and the ticket was a real ticket. He just rubbed his eyes as he signed his name and took his souvenir.

It seemed as if every day I had an adventure driving the Camaro. I thought I would share an incident involving this cruiser on an OUI detail one evening in the Randolph/Pittston area.

I always enjoyed working special details, as I got to concentrate on the detail without being disturbed with other calls. We were given an area to concentrate in and then work the traffic especially hard. The general focus was for OUI enforcement, but I also used all the tools at my disposal to observe and enforce traffic laws. It also provided an opportunity to work with other troopers who patrolled the area to which I was assigned.

On this particular detail, sometime after midnight, I met up with trooper Donnie Armstrong who was patrolling nearby. We pulled our cruisers alongside each other, driver's door to driver's door in a business parking lot off Route 9/Main Street in Randolph. We had been talking with each other for just a few minutes when all of a sudden I heard what I thought was an alarm.

Both of us leaned outside our windows to see if we could hone in on the sound and learn where it was coming from. To me, it sounded like the noise was coming from a building to the south, so I backed out of the parking lot, put the windows down and drove very slowly out of town.

I had gone by multiple businesses and the sound seemed to be getting louder. As I was approaching a service station/auto parts store, a vehicle shot out from behind the service station like a rocket. The dust flew and the vehicle almost went up on two wheels as the driver turned onto Main Street and sped off south on Route 9.

For me, this was pretty exciting. Usually when I got an alarm call, I was at least a half-hour away and they always seemed to be false alarms. But not this time. I was right there and, after observing this vehicle, it appeared this alarm was not going to be false.

As I continued south, it was very clear the alarm was sounding at the business the vehicle had just departed. So with blue lights on, off I went to chase the suspect vehicle.

The suspect vehicle had a little jump on me but certainly not enough. I closed in quickly when the suspect vehicle made a quick left turn onto Kinderhook Street and headed east. The suspect vehicle then started to pick up speed, but it was no match for the Camaro cruiser.

I quickly drove up beside him and lit up the inside of his vehicle with my takedown lights. The operator was a panicking man doing everything he could do to get away. But it wasn't going to happen. He finally looked over at me and gave me an "I give up" look. He pulled over and I pulled in behind him.

I approached the operator with my firearm ready. At the time, all I knew was that this guy might have just committed a felony and who knew what kind of shape he was going to be in. Always prepare for the worst. As I came up beside him and had him place his hands where I could see them, I started asking questions.

"Where are you coming from?" I asked.

"Nowhere."

"Well, I just saw you come out from behind the service station."

"Well, I was going to the bathroom out behind the building," he told me.

"So why is the alarm going off?" I asked.

"I have no idea. But it scared me, so I took off."

"Well, I have another trooper checking the building right now and we'll see if you were peeing outside or inside," I told him. "By the way, why are you sweating so badly?"

The sweat was literally running in streams down his cheeks. As cool as this guy was trying to act, all his bodily functions and actions told me otherwise.

Soon, the other trooper told me that the service station had, in fact, been broken into and someone had entered the building. It was the only way the alarm could go off. Someone had to be inside, not just break the window.

When the suspect heard the news he broke down and confessed that he had, in fact, broken into the service station and the alarm had scared him off after he got inside.

I removed the suspect from his vehicle and started walking him back to my cruiser. All of a sudden, he saw my cruiser and just stopped in his tracks.

"That is what you were chasing me with?" he asked.

"Yes it is," I told him.

"You know, this just isn't my night," he said. "I couldn't have gotten away even if I tried."

I loaded him into the cruiser, met with Trooper Armstrong back at the service station and turned the suspect over to him. He was whisked away to the county lockup in Augusta for burglary and theft. That was the other good thing about details — the case was officially Trooper Armstrong's, and I did not have to do the paperwork.

Just another quiet evening.

We Got 'Em

The news about the kidnapped boy in the Midwest is, of course, maddening. It makes my skin crawl to think what kind of monster would steal a 10-year-old boy. Then the boy was found, along with another boy who had been kidnapped four years earlier. It gave me mixed emotions; was certainly heart-warming they were found alive and well. There are so many other aspects to this type of story, though. You have to think of how parents feel when their child is missing, and then when they are located.

This story is about being with parents when their children were found. Even though it did not involve a kidnapping, missing children are missing children. The anguish that parents endure is horrible.

Late one spring evening, I was called to an old farmhouse in Weeks Mills. The caller was frantic as his two children, ages 10 and 8, were missing. The caller was the father of the children. He called, as his wife was so upset she was unable to. I went to investigate the matter. Of course, my sidekick Game Warden John Ford was with me.

The farm was isolated on a dirt road. Neighbors were quite a distance away. I arrived at the farm and spoke with the parents. The mother was so distraught that she could barely speak. I was told that everything had been fine at the home throughout the day and into the evening.

The father thought the children were upstairs playing and when the parents went to put the children to bed, they couldn't find them. The family dog also was missing, and if there was any consolation for the parents, they were hoping the dog was with the children.

To start this type of investigation, I began from within and worked my way out. The parents had to be questioned and the house had to be searched for signs of the children or suspicious actions.

After the initial investigation, it became apparent the children had wandered off on the property or even farther. The task was to find them before something bad happened to them. To make matters challenging, the parents ran a peat moss farm and in the woods there were deep bogs of peat moss, high ledges and huge drop-offs.

I requested a canine unit and Trooper Tom Bureau came with his dog, Major. Other law enforcement personnel arrived as well.

One requirement of having a canine be effective is to not contaminate the scene. When Trooper Bureau arrived with Major they went right to work. Trooper Bureau asked for someone to run along with them and John volunteered.

I laughed and told John, "You'll never make it back!" John just looked at me with his big nickel-spitting toothy grin and gave me a reply that I can't write here. This, of course, gave him more determination to prove he could run with the dog.

Major immediately got a scent and off they went into the woods. The rest of us scoured the yard and out-buildings to see if we could turn up anything. We found nothing.

Trooper Bureau, Major and John had been gone for some time and things were not looking that good. We kept radio contact with them and set up a command post in the dooryard. It was starting to push midnight, and things were plodding along. Trooper Bureau was searching with Major and John and a small group of police looked around the perimeter of the farm. I kept vigil with the parents in the home.

Many other relatives had shown up and at that time the best bet was to wait on Major. However, in my mind, I was very worried we were not going to be able to locate the children that night, so I started making plans for an all-out search at the first sign of daylight.

Staying with the parents was heart-breaking. To see the anguish on their faces and to see how worried they were defies description. I so wanted everything to go faster and for the children to be found immediately, but it just wasn't so. Minutes turned into hours. Trooper Bureau radioed often and advised me of the very tough terrain. However he felt confident that Major was onto their scent.

It was getting to be about 2 a.m. and I was in my cruiser organizing an early morning search when Trooper Bureau called on the radio. "We got 'em!" he said. "They're about two miles in the woods and they're with their dog!"

"Are they OK?" I asked.

"They're OK and we're on our way out."

I was so excited to hear these children had been found and they were OK. I ran into the house to let the parents know that we had found their children. I had a huge smile on my face as I entered the kitchen. They knew even before I told them.

"Trooper Bureau and Major have found your children. They're OK and they're on their way out right now," I said.

I have never seen such joy on the faces of parents as I did that night. The mom cried with tears of joy. The whole family rejoiced. I got hugged by everyone there. It sure made me feel good to have been a part of finding the children. Of course, it took a long while for Trooper Bureau and the group to make it out. But they finally made it to the farmhouse. To see these children hugged by their parents and relatives was, well, what can you say. It just made me feel good.

The law enforcement group got together outside after the family went inside and Trooper Bureau told us the details of the search. After listening to his and John's story, I realized how lucky we were to find these children alive. The youth had stopped just yards away from a cliff to settle down for the night because they knew how lost they were. If they had gone any farther, who knows what would have happened. The family dog was right with them, keeping them warm and protecting them all the time.

A happy ending to another story.

All the Way to the Supreme Court

When I first came on with the Maine State Police in 1977, the duty was for 24 hours a day, six days a week. The department owned us, and if it needed us on our day off and found us, we had to respond. The secret was to hide very well on days off. We always were needed on holidays, weekends and especially when bad weather was forecast.

I have driven in the absolute worst conditions imaginable. And if a storm was predicted, I could count on the department making sure I would be available and on the road when it arrived.

Sometimes, it didn't make any sense to be out there, as most people figured out that they should stay at home during the worst of times. Then again, other times it paid off to be out there to help stranded motorists and make sure they were safe.

When I was stationed in Greenville, I put a set of issued tire chains in the cruiser. I used them many times. These chains made my cruiser drive like a bulldozer in the worst of conditions. In some blizzards, I could not even see the end of the cruiser hood, and I often wondered what my tracks would look like if someone was following me. I am sure they wandered from snow bank to snow bank.

I must say, though, that in the long run, it was certainly the right thing to do — to be on the roads when the storms hit. Over my career I assisted many a motorist. However, some people weren't all that happy to see me.

This is a story of one of those people.

I had just finished patrolling the northern end of my patrol area and was returning from the Jackman area to Greenville on Route 15. There had been a fair amount of snow, but it was a nice, dry snow and there was no wind. The driving was easy and the roads had just been plowed. Just as I got to Greenville, I thought I would check a few streets, as the local officer had stayed in for the evening. It was well past midnight, and I had just turned onto a side street off the east side of Moosehead Lake.

I followed a set of tire marks that went off the road to the right. There in the ditch was a pickup truck with which I was very familiar. It belonged to a fellow named David, a local from Greenville.

I had known David since becoming a trooper a year earlier. I was quite surprised to see his vehicle in the ditch, as I rarely ever saw him in it as he was almost always inebriated. The vehicle had always been parked in his dooryard when I had to go there. I didn't even think that David had a license.

Knowing who owned the vehicle and knowing the people who he hung around with, I figured that I was probably going to be dealing with someone who had been drinking. After observing the tire marks, it was clear the weather was not the reason the pickup was in the ditch.

I walked up alongside the truck and shined my flashlight into it. There was one person behind the wheel and he was passed out with his head slumped over the wheel.

The pickup was running and I could see the tire marks indicating that he had attempted to drive it out of the ditch but couldn't make it. I also knew the time frame of this accident, as it had stopped snowing within the previous 20 minutes. The tire marks were fresh and had no snow over them.

I checked to see if there were any footprints leading to or from the suspect vehicle. There were none. So I knew the only person involved in this incident would be the man passed out behind the wheel.

I made my way to the driver's door and opened it. The man slumped over the wheel immediately came to and was startled to see me. It was David. He knew me well, and I could tell from his eyes that he was not happy to see me.

I asked David if he was OK, and he said he was. I asked him how he got into the ditch and he immediately denied he had been driving. He told me that some guy he was drinking with at the bar had driven and he was just a passenger.

I asked him where that guy went to and David told me that he took off after the truck got stuck. I then asked David who the guy was and, of course, David told me he didn't know who it was as he had just met him in the bar.

I just kept letting David talk to see how big of a hole he could dig himself. From where I was standing, it was obvious that David was in his normal condition — drunk.

At that time I only needed one question answered: "When was the last time you had anything to drink anyway, David?"

"Oh, I haven't had anything since I left the bar," he told me.

That was all I needed from him. It was important to show that he didn't get stuck, then pull out a bottle of liquor and start drinking after he got stuck. I've had those kind of cases, and they are difficult to prove in court.

I helped David out of the vehicle and placed him into the cruiser. I searched his pickup to see if I could find any bottles of beer or alcohol. I found none, which then strengthened my case.

After the search, I processed David for the offense of operating under the influence. His blood alcohol was very high and his physical characteristics all pointed to someone who was clearly under the influence of alcohol.

He kept warning me that I would never convict him in court for OUI, but I told him I was simply doing my job and it would be up to the court to decide if he was guilty of the offense.

We bantered back and forth for a while — his mild threats went on deaf ears and I was quite confident of the case I had against him. He was summoned to court for an arraignment for the offense of OUI.

I will say that I underestimated my suspect by a lot. From the outside, he appeared to be "just a drunk" who was intoxicated all the time and always around booze. All his friends were drinkers. He lived in a not-too-nice place, and the police seemed to be involved often in his life. I thought it would be an easy case in the court system.

This case was one of those that taught me a lesson.

The first thing David did was hire an attorney — which slows the process to a creep. A whole bunch of motions were filed with the court, evidence was produced and we had to have hearings.

But in the end, a conviction of OUI was found in District Court.

In those days a conviction could be appealed to Superior Court and it was. The jury found him guilty of the OUI a second time. This just seemed to infuriate the attorney and David even more.

The next thing I knew the case was being appealed to the Maine Supreme Court.

Finally, after years of legal wrangling, the Supreme Court ruled on the state's behalf to uphold the OUI conviction.

There were a couple of key pieces of evidence in this case. I had taken the time to observe there weren't any footprints in the fresh snow around the vehicle.

I believe this was the first case of its kind — a conviction due to lack of footprints.

Just another quiet evening.

Where Did He Go?

I attended the retirement dinner for Col. Craig Poulin in Augusta when he departed from the Maine State Police, partly to make sure he was gone but mostly because it was an opportunity to see other troopers that I worked with over the years.

One of the best reasons to attend these functions is to not only pay tribute to the retiree, but to see other co-workers you may not have seen for many years. We get to reminisce and be reminded of many things that we were involved in that we forgot over the years.

While conversing with troopers, I ran into an old friend who used to patrol beside me, Tim Marks. After patrolling in Troop D he transferred to the Turnpike.

"Do you remember the time I had to investigate your crash with the ATV?" he asked.

It all came back in a flash. We both shook our heads in disbelief as to how close two kids were to being injured while trying to get away from the police.

It was about 1 a.m. one morning in the summer of 1988. I was heading north on Route 9/202 going up the east side of China Lake.

I had a ride-along who was interested in law enforcement. It had been a very busy night. After removing a couple of drunk drivers from the road and answering a number of complaints, I was hurrying along. I had to get the rider to a certain location then try to get home for some rest before another detail later that morning.

All of a sudden, out of the darkness a lone headlight was coming at me south on Route 9. It didn't seem right and as I passed the headlight I could see why.

Two ATVs were traveling southbound in the roadway just as fast as they could go. One of the ATVs did not have a light; they were navigating with just one. I slowed down the cruiser and quickly turned to go after them.

I could see they had turned onto the Cross Road which cuts over to the Hanson Road. This road was all gravel and had lots of turns and dips.

Just as I turned onto the road, my headlights picked up one of the ATVs being abandoned right in the middle of the road. The driver ran to jump onto the other ATV.

I narrowly missed the abandoned ATV. I swerved around it and pursued the second ATV with both people on it. The speed limit on this little stretch of road is 35 mph and even that is too fast at some locations on this road.

I quickly caught up to the ATV and clocked it going 55-60 mph. The rider on the back had turned around and was throwing anything he could at my cruiser.

The ATV was skidding all over the road, but I decided to stay behind it as I knew there was no place for him to get off the road and get away from me.

I was close enough to keep him from turning off. The cruiser's blue lights flashed and the siren screamed, but these guys were not going to stop. I was worried that when they got to the Hanson Road they would get into a field and I would lose them.

After a scary wild ride across the Cross Road we came to the T-intersection with the Hanson Road. The ATV skidded through the turn to the right and headed south. I was hot on his tail. This section of road is pretty straight and I thought that this would be the place to get this ATV stopped. The ditches on the left had just been re-dug and the field beyond the ditch was higher than the road.

One technique that always worked well during high-speed pursuits was to "take the road away from the suspect."

I decided to apply this technique. I ran up beside the ATV so it was just off my driver's door. I kept moving over and taking the road away, basically crowding him into the ditch to get him stopped. Our speeds after the turn had slowed and before the speeds picked back up I figured this was the time to get the job done.

I kept closing off the road and eventually the ATV went down into the ditch. What I wasn't aware of, though, was that the driver was going to do whatever he could to get away.

Rather than stop, he accelerated and when he went into the ditch, he started up the other side. But the ground was too steep and in mid-air the ATV did a sideways somersault. The end result was that the ATV landed upside-down on the hood of my cruiser. I could see the passenger doing some mad scrambling to get off my hood and run, but I lost sight of the driver.

My ride-along jumped out of the cruiser and chased the ATV passenger while I jumped out to grab the driver. However, I couldn't find him. I shined my flashlight all over but still could not find the driver.

I could, however, hear him screaming at the top his lungs. I started to run to the front of my cruiser when I noticed a sneaker half-stuck under the cruiser's left front tire.

But there was nobody in the sneaker.

I ran to the front of the cruiser and there, lying on the ground, halfway under the front bumper was the driver.

I grabbed him and stood him up facing me. I never saw anyone so petrified in my life. His eyes were as big as baseballs. I realized he had wet his pants and he was still wetting them as I stood him up. Thinking quickly, I stepped to the side to keep it from getting on me. I immediately recognized the little criminal. He was all of 14 years old and I had already dealt with him and his family many times.

After an investigation, it turned out these kids had stolen both ATVs. They hid them in the woods for the summer and used them only at night to go riding and raise the devil.

The passenger was caught the following day and they were both turned over to their parents and charged with crimes. It certainly was a wild chase for the half-mile it lasted.

As a footnote — the juvenile who was driving continued his life of crime — he later robbed a bank and spent many years in jail for that crime.

Just another quiet evening.

The Night I Met Jeff Parola

This is a story about a young Maine State Police Trooper who made the ultimate sacrifice while serving the citizens of Maine. His name is Jeffrey Parola. Jeff grew up in Dexter and excelled in high school sports. I was told his passion was to someday be a trooper and he followed his dream. He worked for a couple of town police departments, one of them being Hampden, before being hired as a Maine State trooper. He went through the Maine State Police Academy and, upon graduation, was assigned to the Machias area in Washington County.

Everyone knows the best pies in Machias are at Helen's restaurant. Helen's was a favorite spot for troopers to hang out and it so happened that Jeff followed tradition, visiting the restaurant and eating pies. He also ended up dating, and then marrying, the restaurant owner's granddaughter. After a few years in Washington County, Jeff transferred to Troop C in Skowhegan and patrolled the Norridgewock area.

After becoming a trooper, Jeff's next passion was to be part of the elite tactical team or, as some people know it, the SWAT team. This special group of troopers spends a lot of time together training and learning all about each other. Their very lives depend on each other when they face life-threatening situations.

It was one of those life-threatening domestic situations that Jeff was responding to in 1994 when he lost his life. More than 1,800 people attended Jeff's funeral in Waterville. I will never forget marching from the church to the cemetery, following the hearse that was carrying Jeff to his grave. Both sides of Silver Street were lined with mourners and onlookers. Many saluted as we passed by. Many others said, "God Bless you guys." I do not think there were many dry eyes among the troopers or other law enforcement personnel who attended the ceremony.

Jeff was an excellent trooper who did it all. And he was a great person. I remember the first time I met Jeff. It really is quite a story, one that brought me to the edge of my seat, figuratively and literally.

The year was 1988. It was about 1 a.m. when I was called on the radio and told that Hampden police were involved in a high-speed chase southbound on Route 9 going toward Troy and Unity.

At the time I was in Winslow, pulled up alongside a Winslow cruiser talking with a police officer about a particular case we were working together. You just never know which way chases are going to go, so at the time I switched my radio over to Orono and listened to it.

I thought for sure the chase would not make it into Waldo County. Hampden police kept reporting the location of the chase and that it was reaching speeds close to 100 mph. All of a sudden I realized there weren't that many more turnoffs for the suspect to take and the chase might make it to Unity after all.

I bid good night to the Winslow officer and headed up Route 139 toward Unity to set up a road block. Still listening to the chase on the radio, I realized that I did not have time to get to Unity, so I started cutting across back roads to get to Albion to try to get in front of the suspect vehicle.

The radio traffic was extremely exciting as the officer tried to keep up with the speeding vehicle. I learned the officer was chasing a 1979 Chevrolet Camaro with two subjects in it. It was all the officer could do to just stay with it, let alone try to overtake the vehicle and force it off the road.

I kept listening as the chase came into Waldo County, through Troy and into Unity. After it went through Unity, the suspect vehicle did not turn and headed toward Albion on Route 9. I had made the right decision to get to Albion to try to get ahead of the vehicle.

I was traveling the back roads at warp speed, hitting yes ma'ams, trying to keep my head from banging into the ceiling, and squealing tires around all the tight turns.

I could tell it was going to be close whether I could get to Albion in time. I finally made it to the four-way intersection of the Benton Road, Winslow Road and Route 9 on the west side of town.

As I stopped, I looked left. Coming down Main Street was a speeding sports car with blue lights right behind it. I waited about one second before deciding what to do next.

As the Camaro approached me, with the cruiser's blue lights on, I simply drove into the intersection, blocking the Winslow Road and blocking the Benton Road. This would make it extremely difficult for the driver to make the 90-degree turn at the speed he was driving.

And make it, he didn't. The Camaro went into a skid right in front of me, spraying my windshield with small pebbles from the intersection. The driver desperately tried to straighten out the Camaro but it fishtailed several times before going off the right side of the road and sideswiping a utility pole. The pole broke, bringing down wires across Main Street. I was right on the Camaro's tail as I was determined this guy was going no farther!

When he struck the pole it ripped out the rear axle of the Camaro. The driver had no control of how fast or in what direction he was going. The Camaro came back onto the road, skidded onto another lawn and crashed into a neighbor's stonewalled well before coming to a complete stop.

You can guess that I was excited and my adrenalin was pumping pretty hard. I wasn't even thinking about all the downed wires that I dodged as I made my way to the Camaro.

I opened the driver's door and grabbed the kid behind the wheel. I think he thought for one second that he might resist, but that did no good as I pulled him out and took him to the ground with his head right beside the rear wheel.

I had him in a hold around the neck that not even a sumo wrestler could have gotten out of when all of a sudden the car blew up. And when I say blow up, I mean blow up! Apparently, the gas tank had ripped open and gas had poured over the hot exhaust pipes near the rear wheels.

I thought to myself, "This isn't good."

I pulled the kid away from the car and turned him over to the Hampden officer. I can't tell you how excited I was as things unfolded. I think I may have even singed my eyebrows in the mêlée before getting the kid away from the car.

The stonewalled well was close to the home where we landed and I thought it might be a good idea to evacuate the occupant of the house.

The suspect vehicle that was chased.

I ran to the front door of the house and banged on it as hard as I could to awaken the middle-aged couple who lived there. Just then the door flew open and there stood the lady of the house. I knew that I had scared her as she came to the door wearing only her bra and ample granny panties. Well, to say the least, this scared me even more so. I let out a screech and told her she and her husband needed to get out of the house ASAP, but that she had time to put on some clothes. With that warning, I left her and went back to all the excitement on her front lawn.

It turned out the Hampden officer who was chasing these two in the Camaro was none other than Jeffrey Parola. And that was the night I met this outstanding officer and gentleman. I never did ask him what he thought of the whole thing as he took the prisoner and went on his way back to Hampden. He probably didn't want anything more to do with us down here, anyway.

Just another quiet evening!

The Legend

This story is about the night my warden buddy, John Ford, was anointed a "legend in these parts."

It all started one evening when my ride-along partner was none other than John Boy. We sure had fun in those days crisscrossing the county, answering complaints, stopping cars and talking with a lot of people.

It was quite late one night and John and I came upon a van that was all over the road. We clearly needed to stop the vehicle to see if the driver was OK and to see what the problem might be.

During the stop, it was quite apparent the operator was drunk. It was a routine OUI as I put the driver through the process. I had him get out of his van and into the front passenger seat of my cruiser, then asked him questions, had him take a breath test and issued a summons, all the while observing him.

John had taken up his usual spot in the backseat behind the passenger and busied himself with whatever he could find to amuse himself with back there. The OUI suspect was very cooperative and admitted to drinking too much before driving. We treated each other with mutual respect. He knew that I was simply doing my job.

I started to make arrangements with him about what to do with him and his van after we were done. As long as someone was cooperative and I got a promise of no more driving until morning, I usually drove the suspects to their homes and had the vehicles driven to the same location.

I always figured by the time the court system was done with them and then the insurance company boosted their rates, that they had paid enough. They didn't need bail from jail and a towing fee tacked on top of it all.

So it was with this OUI suspect — he was being cooperative and all so I made that particular arrangement. John could drive the intoxicated man's vehicle and I would take him home.

Just then, the OUI suspect realized that someone was in the backseat. He half-turned around in his seat to look at my passenger.

"Who are you?" he asked John.

"I'm John Ford, local game warden," John told him.

Just then the OUI suspect's eyes got even wider and he looked at John with disbelief.

"You're John Ford?" he asked.

"Yup, I am."

All of a sudden, I could see exactly where this was going. The OUI suspect was very impressed that John Ford was riding with me. The suspect turned completely around in his seat and extended his hand toward John.

"I want to shake your hand, Sir. John Ford, why you are a legend in these parts," the OUI suspect told John.

John puffed up like a balloon filled with helium. I could actually see his head swelling. They shook hands for quite some time before the OUI suspect let go.

At that time, all I could do was roll my eyes back in my head. It was hard enough to deal with John, but after this, well, it was going to be torture. I would never hear the end of it and his head would probably be too big to get out of the cruiser. And then I'd be stuck with him in my cruiser.

John and the OUI suspect exchanged pleasantries for quite some time and then John showed a side of himself that few know. John wanted to share his new friend's praise with me. John thanked the suspect for his kind remarks and then asked him what he thought of the trooper who was arresting him.

The OUI suspect asked John, "You mean this trooper right here?"

"Yes, what do you think of my friend, Mark?" John asked.

"Well, he's nothing but an a$$*@#e," the OUI suspect told John.

Well, John got the biggest laugh out of that comment. I was completely stunned as I had just made all the arrangements to save this guy some money and keep him from spending the night in jail.

I guess that was the thanks I got for being nice. So I looked right at my unappreciative OUI suspect and simply asked him, "You know that arrangement we just made about getting you and your van home for the night?"

"Yeah," he recalled.

"Well, you can forget that one. You just earned yourself a one-way ride to the county lockup," I told him. "And we can sit right here while we watch the wrecker come and hook onto your van and haul it off."

I think what I said finally started to sink in as his smirk slowly disappeared from his face.

Just another quiet evening in Waldo County. And guess what, it was a loooong time before I didn't have to hear those words, "You're a legend in these parts," from my old friend, John Ford.

Poor Little Rich Kids

One thing that drives me crazy is seeing the publicity and special treatment that certain people get just because they come from wealthy families.

I always thought that everyone should be treated equally. If you do something wrong and get caught you should be penalized. Period.

During my career, I had the opportunity many times over to deal with people who thought they shouldn't be bothered by law enforcement. And if they were caught, they thought their family's money or influence should take care of it.

I had one case in which a doctor was caught operating under the influence before noon. He had an extremely high blood-alcohol count and caused an accident, crashing head-on into another vehicle. It took me more than two years to get a conviction because he was politically connected and he thought he was going to walk. However, I didn't cave in to pressure and stood firm until I got the rightful conviction.

I could tell many similar stories. Here is one.

In the late 1970s, I was on patrol one evening in the Monson area. I had my sidekick, Deputy Ben Pinkham, with me and we were working the traffic pretty hard on Route 15. While sitting in the firehouse parking lot, two vehicles traveled south through town. They were close together, which told me they were probably traveling as a pair.

As they went by, I recognized both vehicles. The lead vehicle was a small silver sports car owned by the son of a wealthy business owner in a neighboring town. I knew the son quite well and had plenty of dealings with him, mostly bad. He was not afraid to throw his daddy's name and influence in my face. I also knew he was a partier and often was around booze and drugs. He went by the name of Randy.

The second vehicle was owned by a business owner from another town who had not taken a clean breath of fresh air since I had known him. From what everyone had told me, it had been many decades since he had. His name was Bo.

I knew both of these drivers would be good OUI checks, so I followed them south on Route 15 toward Abbot. After leaving Monson on Route 15, the road is hilly but straight for about four miles.

Both vehicles were all over the road so I told Ben we needed to get them both stopped. Up to that point in my career, the following maneuver had worked every time, but it was tricky and could only be done when the suspect vehicles cooperated.

I chose my spot to make the stop, slid up beside the second vehicle and put on my blue lights. Ben lit up the interior of the vehicle and sure enough, there was Bo all alone in the vehicle. He seemed to be concentrating on the car in front of him.

We got Bo's attention and signaled for him to stop. I then proceeded to the lead vehicle with my blue lights on and lit up the interior of that vehicle and identified the driver as Randy.

Randy looked at me, then started to pull over and stop. The tricky part was trying to get the second vehicle to pull over as well.

I followed the lead vehicle onto the shoulder of the roadway, but I stayed out in the lane to try to block the second vehicle from getting around us.

It became obvious that Bo had other plans, though, as he veered way over to the other side of the road. My next thought was to get out of the cruiser and flag down the second vehicle with a flashlight. I rammed the gear shift into park, and opened the door of the cruiser to jump out. That is where the night started its downhill spiral.

Apparently, I did not get the cruiser all the way into park and it rolled forward and bumped the bumper of Randy's vehicle.

There was hardly any contact, but I knew the cruiser did, in fact, touch his car. In the meantime, I jumped into the middle of the road and attempted to stop Bo's vehicle. It was not to be. Bo drove so far to the left that he swerved on the grass on the other side to avoid hitting me. After getting around me, Bo took off, leaving his buddy for me to deal with.

There was no one else available to stop him down the road, so I went back and dealt with Randy. I got him out of his vehicle and placed him in my cruiser. Randy was drunk beyond words. And he had the audacity to try to talk his way out of the arrest.

When he realized I wouldn't change my mind about arresting him, he accused me of running into his car and giving him a severe case of whiplash. Randy went completely limp and said he was suffering from my cruiser striking his vehicle.

I thought the best thing to do was to take him to jail and deal with him there, so off we went to the county lockup in Dover-Foxcroft. Randy was uncooperative all the way to jail and kept threatening that he was going to sue me for injuring him.

We arrived at the jail and I told Randy we had to go inside and get booked. Randy told me he was completely paralyzed from the waist down and could not walk. Despite my persistence, he would not move. So Ben and I each grabbed an arm and dragged him into the booking room of the jail. I knew the whole thing was an act by this poor little rich kid who was trying to get me fired.

Inside, Randy was still uncooperative. He sat in a chair and demanded to talk with his attorney. I told him that he had no right to an attorney unless I was going to question him, and I had no questions to ask him. But he would not hear of it. I kept offering him the blood alcohol test, but he would not answer without conferring with an attorney.

After about 30 minutes of him killing time to try to get his blood alcohol lower, I asked him which attorney he wanted. (I was tired of dealing with him and wanted to get it over with.) Randy gave me the name of an attorney who I knew quite well.

In the meantime my co-worker, Cpl. Paul Davis, showed up to watch the whole spectacle. Paul chuckled about the situation and when Randy asked for a particular attorney, Paul agreed to disturb him at that very early hour. We could all tell the attorney was not pleased to be called and he was unhappy when we told him about the game that Randy was playing about being paralyzed.

The attorney requested to speak with Randy, but the phone would not reach where Randy was perched. We told Randy he had to come to the phone if he wanted to speak with his attorney. So, Randy got out of his chair, slid on the floor and crawled over to the phone, pulling himself along by his elbows.

We shook our heads as Randy told the lawyer a great big fairy tale about being run over by the cruiser and being paralyzed.

After Randy spoke with his attorney, he handed the phone to me. The lawyer requested that I call an ambulance and have his client taken to the hospital to be examined. The attorney said I could request that Randy's blood alcohol be tested at the hospital. Even though I told the attorney that his client was faking, he asked me to do this at the client's expense. I told him I would.

Guess what?

While waiting for the ambulance, the driver of the second vehicle, Bo, arrived at the county jail. He strolled in and said he wanted to bail his friend Randy out of jail. Bo was sloshed. He could barely speak and he leaned against the walls for support. Deputy Pinkham and I spoke with him in the entrance of the jail.

Ben asked, "How much have you had to drink anyway, Bo?"

"*Drink*? I don't drink!" Bo replied.

"You don't *drink*!?!" asked Ben, "We'd have to set you on fire to dry you out!"

After realizing that Bo had a driver, and we could not arrest him for the earlier incident, he was told to leave the complex, as his friend was being taken away and would not be able to be bailed out.

At the hospital, the emergency room doctor examined Randy. I filled the doctor in on what happened and gave him my opinion. The doctor said he would get a reflex out of him and that I shouldn't worry. I observed from the other room and watched as the doctor did a few things that would have lifted me right off the table. But it didn't even budge Randy.

I admit I was concerned. There was no way my cruiser bumping into his bumper did any damage to anyone or anything. But Randy definitely took the show to another whole level. After failing to get any type of reflex from Randy, the doctor drew his blood and told me that he would keep Randy for the night and that he would call me if there was any change.

I was in complete shock at what I had seen and heard. I just knew this kid was faking, but he was fooling everyone.

I took the blood alcohol test from the doctor, and Ben and I left the hospital for the North Woods. I could not help but think that I was in some kind of trouble as I headed home.

Now the kicker. Later that morning, I received a call from the doctor. He chuckled as he told me what happened. Apparently, when Randy woke up, he was startled, jumped off the emergency bed and screamed to one of the nurses, "Where the hell am I?"

When he was told where he was Randy yelled, "To hell with that!" and ran out of the hospital.

Guess he wasn't paralyzed after all.

Just another quiet evening.

Topless in February

This incident occurred one frigid February evening when I had my usual sidekick, John Ford, along for the ride. It was definitely a night wherein most people stayed home and stoked their stoves with wood to stay warm.

I remember my cruiser having a hard time staying warm enough to keep the windows from frosting over. The defroster had to work overtime so we could see. The tires never warmed up and they thumped all night long.

Believe me when I tell you it was cold. John and I had not seen a vehicle on the road for more than four hours. So rather than look for bad guys, the night turned out to be more of a "check and make sure no one is stranded" night.

John and I had checked many of the roads throughout the county and had found no stranded motorists. We had not even had a call, and all seemed really quiet.

It was getting to be about 2 a.m. and we were checking a few more roads before calling it a night and heading to our own homes. I was certainly looking forward to getting into a nice warm bed for the rest of the night and I am sure John was also, as he kept telling me to point the cruiser for Brooks.

I told John, just a couple of more roads. We were heading south on the South Freedom Road when all of a sudden we met a vehicle traveling north. Meeting a vehicle is no big deal, except that night it was unusual due to it being so cold. But when we met it and saw what it was for a vehicle, John and I looked at each other in complete disbelief.

"Did you see what I saw?" I asked John.

"Why don't you tell me what you saw, then I'll tell you," he replied.

"I think I saw an old military Jeep with the windshield down," I said.

"Yep, that's what I saw!" John squealed. "He's gotta be drunk!"

"Yup, he's gotta be drunk. He deserves to be stopped for just being stupid."

I turned around my cruiser and went after the Jeep. Catching up with it a short distance away, I turned on the blue lights and the driver of the Jeep pulled right over and stopped.

Believe it or not, we were right. It was an old M*A*S*H*-type Jeep and the windshield was folded down so the driver had no protection from the elements. Basically a topless Jeep.

From where John and I were seated we could see the driver was alone and had what looked like a lot of ice-fishing gear thrown into the back of the Jeep. I approached the driver or what I thought was the driver. His head was completely white from the cold. It was like his whole face was crystallized. And he was stiff as a board.

However, I couldn't tell if he was stiff from the cold or all the booze he had drank. Being in a hurry to get back into the warm cruiser, John and I helped the driver out of the seat and into the cruiser. He clearly needed help anyway and I did not want to spend any more time out there than I had to.

After getting the driver into my cruiser and directing the warm air vents directly onto him, the man's face started to thaw out. He could form a few words and it became obvious the booze was taking over from the cold.

"Are you crazy?" I asked him. "Do you know how cold it is?"

"Oh yeah. I've been ice-fishing all day and putting the whiskey right to me. Don't feel a thing!" he told me.

The drunk driver, Rusty, said he had had a wonderful day but it looked like I was going to ruin it for him. I told Rusty that we would have to go through the OUI process, and he would have to take a breath test. I told him if need be, I would summons him and get him and his vehicle to a safe place. Rusty was all set with the process and actually appreciated what we were doing. However, I think John caught on immediately to what I was doing and wasn't quite so appreciative.

Whenever I have a rider along with me, one of the duties I give them is to drive OUI suspects' vehicles to their homes. The exciting part for the riders was they never knew what kind of vehicle they would get to drive. It could be as nice as a Cadillac or as bad as a multi-colored, engine-skipping, door-missing Yugo. Come to think of it, I can't remember riders driving home too many Cadillacs.

"You think I'm going to drive that Jeep, Nickerson?" asked John.

"He just lives about five miles from here, Johnny. Won't you drive it to his house?" I asked him.

"No g*&^%m way I'm driving that vehicle one foot," John told me.

To make a long negotiation short, John finally gave in and drove the Jeep about 100 feet up the road and parked it in a driveway where Rusty knew the people.

I've had a lot of people swear at me in this line of work, but I don't think anyone ever used such colorful words as John did that night after driving that Jeep 100 feet along the road to park it.

I, of course, had to stay with the prisoner in my cruiser for emergency reasons. It was a long time before John let me forget about that particular night.

Thinking about it today sure gives me shivers down my back and cools me right off. I wonder if John remembers it as well.

Just another quiet and cold evening in Waldo County.

Have a Seat

Being a trooper in the North Woods around Moosehead Lake was, at times, like living in the old Wild West.

I remember reading in the 1970s that, at the turn of the 20th century, Greenville was one of the three most-dangerous places to live in the United States. Even in the late '70s, I could easily understand why. It was still clearly the edge of the frontier.

Several railroads came together at Greenville Junction on Moosehead Lake, so people arrived from many locations. The main industry was logging. Men would go into the woods and stay all winter. It was a place for hunting, trapping, fishing and exploring. It truly was and is a unique place.

By the time I made it in to Greenville in 1977, things had changed, but very slowly. Men no longer went into the forest for whole seasons, but they still went into the woods from Sunday night until Thursday. There was a saying when I was a trooper that loggers came out of the woods Thursday for three things — to drink, fight and, for lack of a better word, have "relations."

The town's population was about 2,000 year-round residents. Greenville also boasted eight working and very busy bars that served a lot of alcohol. Compare that to Waldo County. There were maybe only eight bars in the whole county at that time. So you can imagine what kept me busy as a trooper in the region — alcohol-related incidents.

Being called to a bar usually meant one thing. The owner wanted someone removed and calling the police was a last resort. Most of the time, bar owners policed their own matters, but when something didn't go right or the way they wanted it to, they called the police. Walking into a crowded barroom alone to remove a drunk could be a little intimidating — especially when wondering if other patrons might turn if I didn't handle it all that peacefully.

One particular bar in the junction, the Longbranch— where loggers frequently hung out—had a rough reputation. The building had been there for almost 100 years. The bartender and owner was a woman, and she was as tough as any man I had ever met. I heard that one night she threw a man through the front picture window. So whenever she called for the police, I knew my hands were going to be full.

This is the story of one of those bar brawls to which I responded one night. Now remember, I was in my early 20s and not much scared me. I would wade into about anything and try to take care of it the best I could.

The person I had to deal with was a local who was very well known by the local constabulary. First of all, he was huge. And he wasn't fat. He was as big as a gorilla and probably stronger than one.

Fortunately for me, the trooper who patrolled there before me had laid him out with a Kel-light (a six-cell steel flashlight) right over the old noggin. So this guy, we'll call him Gus, seemed to know how far he could go before getting struck again with a Kel-light. So he, somewhat, respected troopers.

I was told that he wasn't a bad guy when he was sober. But I also had heard that when he was drinking, and when his eyes were going in different directions, that I should not stand in front of him.

I had to deal with Gus on many different occasions, and for the most part I had built at least a somewhat respectable relationship with him. He understood when I had to arrest him, and he had never given me any problem.

On this particular night, I received a call at home from a bar owner. He told me he needed me at his place ASAP as Gus was drunk, ripping bar stools out of the floor and throwing them at people in the bar. The owner was petrified that someone was going to get hurt. I told him I would be right over to see what I could do. The owner said to come in the back door as he didn't want Gus to see the police coming.

On the way over, I called local officer Mickey Squiers and told him what was up.

All he could say was, "Oh no." But he reluctantly said he would be on his way to back me up. I arrived at the back kitchen door and met the bar owner inside the kitchen.

The owner's name was Ron. All Ron kept saying was, "Mark, please don't get hurt. All I want is for you to go and approach him, and tell him that you will take him home. I don't want you to arrest him, just get him home."

I could hear Gus screaming in the other room for someone to challenge him. Obviously, no one was taking him up on it. Ron also told me that he had installed the bar stools with four bolts each through the hardwood floor.

Ron thought they were immovable, but Gus had proven him wrong. Ron told me that Gus was ripping them right out of the floor. Just as I was asking Ron if he knew what had upset Gus, the double doors flew open and in came Gus.

And, yes, his eyes were twirling in different directions. I bristled up and was getting ready for an onslaught. My six-cell flashlight was cocked behind my back.

Instead, Gus took one look at me, stopped, hung his head and said, "I know, I know. I did wrong tonight. But what would you do, Mark, if some guy put his hand on your wife's knee and made a pass at her?"

"Probably the same thing that you're doing, Gus," I told him.

"I knew you'd see it my way," Gus said.

"However," I said, "tonight is all over, and Ron here wants me to get you home before someone gets hurt."

"Well, I can't drive home with you here," Gus laughed.

"How about I take you home and that will take care of everything, Gus?"

"You'll do that for me, Mark?"

"Of course I will. Let's go."

And with that Gus and I went right out the back door, got in my cruiser and I took him home. When he got out of the cruiser, he even thanked me for not arresting him. I told him he needed to thank Ron and to apologize to him for ripping up the barstools.

"I'll do one better, I'll fix them for him," Gus said.

And he did.

Afterward, I breathed a big sigh of relief that it turned out the way it did. Nobody got hurt, and when I came face-to-face with the most dangerous man in the area in his worst condition, he backed down.

Just one of many bar brawls I dealt with in my five years in the Moosehead Lake area.

Legendary Trooper Dave Giroux

In 1977, when I went through the Maine State Police Academy, self-defense tactics were a major part of our training. Our instructor was an oversized man by the name of Dave Giroux. He was larger than life in every way, but he also had a soft side.

Here are a few stories about this incredible man that I want to share.

Dave was a Maine State Trooper assigned to the Academy, and he ran the Municipal Academy. He was 6-foot-3, bald and weighed about 250 pounds. He carried himself in a way that indicated he was in extremely good physical condition.

He was not one of those gym rats with big rippling muscles and a flat stomach. He was very unassuming yet he had a physically intimidating presence. Our class was informed that Dave was a five-time New England heavyweight Jiu-Jitsu champion and he was going to train us in self-defense tactics.

When we stretched, he reminded me of Buddha sitting on the ground with his legs crossed. The stories we heard about this man while he patrolled the roads of Maine were legendary. The stories ranged from his removal of uncooperative suspects from vehicles, to assisting other agencies, to the Poland Spring raid in '72 when he took an immense oak door off its frame, to retrieving an American flag being disrespected by protestors at Seabrook Nuclear Power Plant in New Hampshire. People who did not cooperate with this man paid a huge price.

One thing I appreciated about Dave was that his teaching was hands-on. When he showed us a tactic, he used a cadet as an example. He always asked for a volunteer but after watching the punishment he put some of the volunteers through, after a short while, no one volunteered anymore. So Dave would pick someone. I tried to make myself as invisible as possible when

Dave Giroux

he was looking for someone to grab. But by the end of my Academy class, we were down to 16 cadets and I knew I wouldn't be able to avoid the punishment forever.

One afternoon, Dave was demonstrating how to remove a suspect from a vehicle, and he demonstrated a different technique on each cadet. Somehow, I had dodged being the suspect until the end. By that time, I had seen a lot of different ways he had used to get people out from behind the steering wheel. After all that observing, I thought for sure I would be able to resist anything that he did to me. It was my turn, and he told me to get behind the wheel. As I sat there, he told the rest of the class that he would demonstrate how to remove a suspect from a vehicle using only two fingers.

I chuckled to myself as I thought that it would be impossible. I thought I was about to be the only one in the class whom Dave could not remove from the vehicle. Dave ordered me to brace myself as best I could and not let go.

He then ordered me to get out of the vehicle, which I refused to do. He opened the door and positioned himself in a way that kept the door open and he leaned in facing me. He reached in with his left hand, grabbed me right under the nose and squeezed. Tears ran down my cheeks. I was squirming trying to get away and howling due to some of the worst pain I'd ever felt in my life.

Dave then lifted me out of the seat and brought me out of the car quicker than I could have ever thought possible. Once outside, he held me in the same position and I stood on my tippy toes, still screaming in pain.

He kept talking to the other cadets to make sure they understood the position of the grab and what it was doing to me. He finally let go and it was hours before I got any feeling back in my upper lip. So much for being an immovable object.

There was another exercise Dave taught us that really opened my eyes. And I used it many times on the road throughout my career. Not by choice, but because of circumstances.

Dave had a way of showing us things before explaining them to us. One afternoon on the front lawn of the Academy he lined up two of us and told us to race to the street and back. The first one back would get into the lower position of a wrestling match. The loser would get the upper position.

Once the race was over and the two cadets were in position, he yelled, "Go!" Everyone looked at each other wondering what he wanted. Then he yelled, "Wrestle until someone is pinned!"

This taught us that apprehension of a suspect was not over until the suspect was handcuffed. We had to make sure we have enough strength to handcuff our suspect and not completely tire ourselves out in the foot chase. Most suspects who ran were not going to give up just because we caught them. It was clearly an eye-opener for me.

After leaving the Academy, I had many years on the road and each year we got law updates and training on new equipment at the Academy. It was during one of those in-service training classes that I had the opportunity to train again with Dave. A new style of Mace was being introduced and we had to be doused with the chemical to experience what it felt like to be sprayed.

Most of us took the squirt in the face, felt the immediate effects then dunked our heads in a bucket of water to start the cleansing process.

That stuff immediately blinded me, and the burning sting of the chemical made it impossible to breathe. It takes the fight out of most people, for sure.

Then it was Dave's turn. The trainer stood in front of Dave and gave him a healthy dose of the pepper spray. Rather than just standing there and feeling the effects of the chemical, Dave blindly charged the trainer like he was in a rage. The trainer simply stepped to the side and Dave, wildly swinging his arms trying to grab him, missed.

This was another demonstration that clearly opened my eyes and taught me to expect the unexpected. Afterward, I could see the trainer take a deep sigh of relief that he had had the wise sense to step aside and not get caught in the death grip of Dave Giroux.

Dave Giroux truly was an extraordinary man who had an exemplary career. His training undoubtedly gave many officers the upper hand while dealing with violent offenders and prevented many injuries to those officers. Sadly, he passed away after a bout with cancer at a young age. His status and reputation as a Maine State Police trooper will live on through the annals of the Maine State Police.

Spiked

In the early 1990s, our department was looking for better ways to stop fleeing suspect vehicles. High-speed chases were, and still are, one of the most dangerous activities in which an officer can get involved. When I went through the academy, I was taught different methods of stopping fleeing vehicles. Most involved using a roadblock — placing a cruiser ahead of the suspect vehicle. Not only was this dangerous for the officers, but even if no one got hurt, the cruiser was usually demolished if the suspect did not stop.

Finally, a retired police officer invented the spike mat. It seemed like many products appeared simultaneously on the market and our department tested different versions of spike mats, spike sticks and other devices.

Around 1994, the Maine State Police purchased spike mats for every department so just about everyone had one in the trunk. I was pretty fortunate to have been a trainer in the use of the spike mat while instructing the Emergency Vehicle Operators Course, so I had lots of practice throwing it.

Let me describe this piece of equipment. The spike mat comes in a very handy, slim, briefcase-looking case and fits in the trunk of a cruiser. We are trained to store it in our trunk so that it can be easily located, quickly removed and placed on the ground.

When opening the case to remove it, the spike mat is in a position so the throwing hand is on the rope side and can quickly deploy the mat across the road. The mat is folded up in the case and when the mat is thrown, it looks like a whole bunch of scissors tied together that are opening. Police have to don gloves when handling the mat, as it has 100-plus needlelike spikes.

When a vehicle drives over the mat, the spikes puncture the tires and stay in the tires. The spike is hollow, which allows the air to release from the tire in a controlled deflation so the operator does not lose control of the vehicle.

On the EVOC range, we tested the spike mat several times at varying speeds to see how a vehicle handles after the tires are punctured, so I had good working knowledge of this piece of equipment.

However, there was still an extremely dangerous element to this whole procedure which came to light in Maine and other states. The dangerous part is deciding where to take cover from the suspect vehicle.

Some officers were getting hurt due to not taking appropriate cover. There is a lot to think about whenever deploying the spike mat. Not only did we have to worry about being far enough ahead so that we had time to stop, get out and deploy the mat, we also had to find a place to take cover from being run over. Then we had to pull the mat out of the way so the pursuing cruiser did not get spiked, as well.

With all that said, here is my story. It was July 4, 1996. I started work early to prepare my cruiser for a couple of parades. For some reason, my cruiser, a 1996 red fully marked Camaro, seemed to be in great demand for parades.

With all the holiday activities and other duties it turned out to be a busy day. I was looking forward to having the evening off and taking my son to see the fireworks in Winslow. He was

2, and I was anxious to see his reaction to all of the colors bursting in the sky. I had to work several hours past my quitting time of 4 p.m. and was finally getting home around 8 p.m. Just as I was arriving home, however, Maine State Police in Augusta advised all units in Waldo County that there had been an armed robbery in Belfast. A description of the suspect vehicle was given, as was a possible direction it had taken. Trooper Tom Ballard spotted the vehicle traveling west on Route 3, flipped on his blue lights and the suspect vehicle momentarily pulled over. Before Trooper Ballard could proceed with the felony stop, the suspect sped off with Trooper Ballard once again in pursuit.

I had just pulled into my driveway and told my family that I had to go. I hollered out my window that I would find them later at the fireworks.

As I drove south I was making plans on where to set up the spike mat. I decided on the divided highway in South China. It would give me good vision, still give the suspect an element of surprise, and keep oncoming traffic on the other side of the median. Listening to the chase come across Route 3 certainly peaked my adrenalin. It seemed that even the Camaro could not get me there fast enough.

I finally got into position and set a roadblock with my Camaro, which funneled the suspect vehicle to the right where it would then run over the mat.

Then-Sgt. Craig Poulin also arrived and set up his cruiser in the roadblock. I had enough time to set up, divert traffic, and when the suspect vehicle came into sight, I ran for cover.

All I could picture in my head was the bad guy would leave the road and try to run me over. But everything worked according to the plan. The suspect vehicle came into the roadblock at a very high rate of speed, veered right and ran right over the mat. I knew I had gotten him as I could hear the air hissing out of his tires as he drove away.

The mat was pulled out of the way and the two cruisers in pursuit continued chasing the bad guy for about another 500 yards, where he went off the road. He was arrested at gunpoint without incident and was locked up at the Waldo County Jail.

I have to admit that it was exciting to watch and be involved in the chase. When things like that happen and the bad guy is caught, locked up and no one is hurt — well, that is a win-win for everyone, except the bad guy.

Right after the guy was lugged off to jail, Trooper Tim Marks retrieved my spike mat and refilled the missing spikes.

We all cleared the scene and I rushed to Winslow to try to find my family at the fireworks. Try as I might, I was not able to locate them and the fireworks were over. So I headed home, getting there about 10:30 p.m.

It was about 11 p.m. when the phone rang. It was again State Police Augusta, this time advising me that Trooper Brenda Coolen was involved in a chase, and they had just turned onto the North Dixmont Road and were heading toward Troy.

I jumped off the couch and into my cruiser and headed that way. Just as I was coming down the steep hill on Route 220 in Troy by the sand pile, I could see blue lights flashing in the sky over the horizon.

I advised Trooper Coolen of my location and that I would be setting up the mat right in the intersection by the sand pile. I got there just in time and threw the mat. I had about a three-second wait before the speeding pickup truck flew over the mat and continued on, albeit with hissing tires.

The driver of the pickup just barely made it to the top of the hill before he too went off the road with three flat tires. He was so drunk he kept asking what happened to his tires. That suspect was promptly arrested and carted off to jail in Trooper Coolen's cruiser.

After that second vehicle was spiked, I contacted Trooper Marks and thanked him profusely for reloading the spike mat.

That would have been a disaster if I had not had enough spikes in the mat to flatten the tires of the second suspect vehicle. The ironic thing about the mat is this: I carried it in my trunk for about 12 years before I finally retired. I never used it before July 4, 1996, used it twice the evening of July 4, 1996, and never used it again for the rest of my career. But I knew it was there and I knew it worked just fine.

Just another quiet evening in Waldo County.

Shootout in Bangor

2007 was the 70th anniversary of the Al Brady gang's shootout with the FBI, Maine State Police and the Bangor Police Department.

As a young boy I saw historical photos of this event. I always was intrigued by the thought of such a thing happening in Maine. It was hard to imagine a shootout could erupt and dead bodies would lie on a street in Bangor. But I guess that was the only way to deal with such desperadoes during that era.

I learned from a trooper friend in the town of Lincoln that a movie production company was going to recreate the incident and shoot a documentary about it. The trooper, Tom Fiske, who studies and participates in a lot of police history for the state of Maine, was asked to take part in the documentary.

He was chosen to be one of the bad guys. Tom told me the production company was looking for cars from that era to make the street look as authentic as possible.

Well, that gave me an idea. I've got an old friend in Unity by the name of Babe Tozier — also known as Unity's mayor. Babe has a collection of cars from the 20s and 30s, and I thought he might be interested in taking one to Bangor to be in the parade and the street scene.

Anyone who knows the Babe can understand his answer. "Ayuh, that would be fun, Markie," he said, then added his trademark laugh, "Hehe, hehe."

Babe told me he remembered his parents talking about the incident when it actually happened in 1937.

We made a plan to get involved in the documentary. The Babe and I selected his blue 1933 Pontiac sedan with a straight 8. Babe purchased fake bullet holes to place on the windows, and we arranged the particulars. I thought this would be a wonderful experience for my son to witness as well. So my son Max, retired Game Warden Lt. Bill Allen and I rode to Bangor in Babe's 1933 Pontiac, with Babe behind the wheel sporting his FBI cap.

Babe Tozier's '33 Pontiac with fake bullet holes.

Babe wanted to give us plenty of time to make the trip, so we met at his house about two hours before we had to be in Bangor. The gas tank was full and a case of oil was in the back seat with Max and I. The road to Bangor from Unity is actually a pretty good highway, but it wasn't too many miles before I realized our grandparents didn't have it too easy in the vehicle department. Riding in the old car made Route 9 feel like a Jeep trail.

After what seemed like a long journey, we made it to the staging area for the parade in Bangor. We parked alongside the Penobscot River on Railroad Street with about 30 other antique vehicles.

While we were waiting for the parade to travel to the "crime" scene, a newer vehicle pulled up. A distinguished-looking, well-dressed gentleman with white hair emerged from the passenger seat and asked Babe, "Where did you get that FBI cap?"

His name was Col. Walter R. Walsh — and he was one of the FBI agents seriously wounded in the 1937 shooting. The 100-year-old man is the lone survivor of that shootout.

What a wonderful surprise. He was quickly surrounded by other people as everyone wanted to listen to what he had to say. Even though his memory had faded some, he was spry and enjoyed the attention. As his sons were attempting to get him back into the car so they could get to the scene, Babe took a picture of Col. Walsh with Max and I. What an honor.

Walter Walsh, right, 100, was the FBI agent who was shot and seriously wounded in 1937 during the shootout with the Brady Gang. Also pictured are Mark Nickerson and his son, Max Nickerson.

The colonel was whisked away and as the lead cars were escorted onto Main Street, guess what happened? Yup, a train came — all 80 cars of it — and the back half of the parade was cut off.

We thought for sure we were going to miss the whole thing, however we lucked out and after parking, we observed the shootout being re-created right on the streets of Bangor.

The bad guys donned long coats and fedoras and rode in a 1937 Buick. The license plate was Ohio YK-747 — exactly as it was in 1937. Watching the scene unfold was uncannily eerie, as we knew what was about to happen to these guys as they came to pick up their new Tommy gun at Dakin's Sporting Goods store.

We watched intently as the shootout was recreated and two of the three men were gunned down and fell dead. They were then scooped up, placed in a hearse and carted off to the morgue.

After observing the activities, the four of us made it back to the old car. With Babe behind the wheel, we set off for the journey back to Unity. What a great, memorable day for us all to see history recreated.

Al Brady is carried to the hearse.

Meet You at the Monument

It was a beautiful evening in the late spring of 1984. I picked up my rider for the evening, Deputy Rod Sienkiewicz, from his home in Freedom and we headed off for a night of patrolling Waldo County.

Rod often rode along with me. He was great company and a great backup if things didn't go quite the way they were supposed to. I had a new 1984 Chevy Impala cruiser. Although they were good all-around cruisers, they lacked the speed we were used to having.

Rod lived on a back road in Freedom. After I picked him up, we were approaching Route 137 from a side road and observed a motorcycle go screaming by. The motorcycle operator never saw us. I looked at Rod and asked him, "Did you see that bike?"

"I sure did," he said. "He must be doing at least 70."

The speed limit was 25 mph. I knew the operator had not seen me, so I would have the element of surprise and be able to sneak up behind him. This worked absolutely perfectly as I ever-so-slowly crept in behind the motorcycle.

By the time I had caught up and clocked the motorcyclist, he was skipping along at about 90 mph. The cyclist still didn't know I was behind him, and I had built enough of a case to pull him over and make an arrest. I told Rod to hang on, as we had no idea what the guy would do when the blue lights came on.

The time came to put on the blue lights. Nothing happened — which did not surprise me. I knew the cyclist was paying close attention to his driving and not what was behind him. To get his attention, I sounded my siren. He turned around, looked at the cruiser, then turned back around, leaned lower on his bike and left me in his dust.

"Here we go, Rod. Hang on," I said and then watched as both of Rod's hands gripped the dashboard. He was hanging on for dear life.

The cruiser lacked the speed needed for such a chase. I kept the bike in sight as he turned south on the South Freedom Road. I finally closed the gap and it seemed we were just hitting the high spots of the road as we careened along at more than 110 mph.

I called State Police Headquarters, as all chases were monitored. I also notified my supervisor. Anyone familiar with the road knows that several roads branch from it. If I was to catch this guy, I needed to keep him on this road so a roadblock could be set up ahead.

As luck would have it, Trooper Greg Myers was coming out of Augusta on Route 3 and he quickly headed toward Palermo.

I chased the motorcycle, staying just feet off his rear wheel. Rod clung to the dashboard.

I could tell by the motorcyclist's actions that he was looking for a back road to get away from me. Finally, an opportunity came for him — the Level Hill Road. I could see he was preparing to turn left onto it.

I did not let that happen. As he slowed to turn, I quickly veered left and blocked off the road. He actually turned into my right fender and had to kick off from it to stay upright. This forced him to stay on the South Freedom Road. He again took off quickly and left me behind ... for a bit. I was able to catch up with him fairly quickly and block off the next road, too.

I knew Trooper Myers had made it to the monument in Palermo and was setting up a roadblock. It was imperative I keep the motorcyclist on this road. Our speeds picked up to the point that I knew he was going to stay straight and take his chances at the end of it on which way to go.

We made it to the monument in record time. I think we traveled 13 miles in 7 minutes. Rod had turned pale white but was still encouraging me to get this guy.

When the monument came into sight, there sat Trooper Myers' cruiser with its blue lights flashing. He was standing outside ready to take whatever action was needed.

Then the motorcyclist made his mistake. He slowed considerably as if to ask himself, "Where do I go now?"

That was all I needed. He was going slow enough for me to end the chase. I pulled up beside him, and Rod opened his door and dumped the motorcycle and its driver to the ground.

We both bailed out of the cruiser and pounced on him. I was very anxious to see who we had been chasing. I kept trying to get his helmet off, but it would not come off, try as I might. Finally, Trooper Myers came over and told me to undo the strap before I removed the helmet. I guess you could say I was full of adrenalin.

He turned out to be a teenager from Liberty with a new motorcycle. He thought he would terrorize the county on it. The teenager was arrested, placed into Trooper Myers' cruiser and transported to Waldo County Jail.

When the bike was dumped, some damage was done. Hopefully, it would be a while before it was roadworthy again.

After the suspect was carted off to jail, I called for a wrecker. The wrecker arrived and we commenced to clean up the area. There was still a fair amount of personnel around. And then, out of nowhere, an elderly gentleman walked up to me.

"You see that house right there across the street?" he asked me.

"Yes I do," I told him as I looked toward an older well-kept stately home near the intersection.

"Well, let me tell you something. I have lived in that home for 83 years and this is the most exciting thing I have ever seen in my life from that window. Thank you."

With that, he chuckled, shook my hand and wandered back to his house.

Just another quiet evening in Waldo County.

Your Name Was What?

It was a Saturday night in late spring. I was working the roads looking for OUIs and other violations. I had a rider along, as having someone to talk with made the night go by quicker.

I planned my evening so that around bar-closing time, I would be driving toward the city of Waterville and meeting vehicles headed into the rural areas for which I was responsible. I was in Fairfield driving toward Waterville and it was prime OUI time.

While I was traveling south on Route 201 an oncoming vehicle seemed to be having difficulty navigating in the northbound lane. There was a median between the lanes and the vehicle had one set of wheels up on the median. As I passed it I watched it go off the median and weave its way to the sidewalk.

I flipped around and came up behind it. The vehicle was all over the road, weaving back and forth and traveling slow. There were a lot of people in the vehicle and they had no idea I was behind them, watching.

I came up beside the suspect vehicle to identify the driver and then I turned on the blue lights. The vehicle kept going for a short distance as though the driver was thinking about taking off but apparently he thought better of it and pulled over. The vehicle went up over the sidewalk before pulling into a parking lot and coming to a stop.

With all of the passengers, I had to pay attention in case of an attempted switch-around. I quickly ran up to the driver's door just as the driver was attempting to jump into the back seat. I opened the door, grabbed the driver by his belt and pulled him out of the car. He was as drunk as someone could be and clearly in the partying mood.

Everyone in the vehicle was joking and laughing and feeling quite good. I then recognized the group — it was a family that I dealt with often. And it was such a large family that I couldn't keep all the names straight. I knew their last name well though. We'll call them the Smiths.

I brought "driver" Smith back to my cruiser after handcuffing him, then went back to the suspect vehicle to gather names of the others. I knew three of the men were brothers and they often used each other's name when stopped by the police. The names I got were John Smith, Jerry Smith and a couple of women's names.

I got back into my cruiser and started gathering information on the suspect. I asked him his name and he told me he was John Smith.

In the back seat my ride-along coughed to get my attention. I was informed it wasn't John Smith in the front seat but Jim Smith. My ride-along knew the family quite well. I chuckled to my suspect and informed him that his brother back in the car had already told me he was John.

"No, no." Jim told me, "I'm John, that's Jim up in the car."

"Uh huh. Got any identification on you?" I asked.

"Of course not, but I'm telling you I'm John Smith," he said.

Then I remembered something about Jim Smith — he had his name tattooed on his upper left arm. I had him take off his jacket and I slowly raised his T-shirt sleeve and there it was, staring me right in the eye. "J-I-M."

"Now, let's try this one more time. Your name was what?"
I asked.

"How did you know about the tattoo?"

"You just never know who tells us things," I told him as I placed him under arrest for OUI, driving with a suspended license and giving a false name to a law enforcement officer.

Jim's girlfriend came up to the cruiser window and asked what was going on. Jim told her that my ride-along had ratted him out. Jim and his girlfriend continued to talk while I got out to make arrangements with the other family members about the vehicle.

All of a sudden, I heard the most awful screaming and commotion at the side of my cruiser. Jim's girlfriend was throwing punches at my ride-along through the rear window of the cruiser.

I ran over to the cruiser, grabbed Jim's girlfriend by her coat collar and yanked her away from the cruiser so she couldn't throw any more punches. Apparently, I yanked way too hard because when she landed on the pavement, her jacket and shirt were in my hands. She was lying face down wearing pants and a bra.

I quickly handcuffed her, put her coat back on and threw her in the backseat of the cruiser with my ride-along. I then carted both Jim and his honey to the county jail. She was charged with assault and providing a false name to a law enforcement officer as well.

Isn't it amazing how people can't remember their names very well?

Just another quiet evening.

Get Off My Porch!

One of the most scenic rides during the fall foliage season is along Route 201 from Moscow to Jackman and over to Moosehead Lake on Route 15. I discovered this while patrolling in the late 1970s and early '80s. Each year it was a ritual for me to pick up my friend, Chief Maxim "Mickey" Squiers of the Greenville Police Department, and go for this ride as we patrolled the area. We started in Greenville, headed north on Route 15 through Rockwood, to Jackman, and to the Canadian border, then headed south on Route 201 to Bingham. In Bingham, we cut across Route 16 into Abbott Village, turned left onto Route 15 and headed back to Greenville.

The scenery was breathtaking as we traveled along the lakes and through the mountains. It was clearly one of my favorite and most enjoyable patrol rides. It was hard to imagine this was work. Of course, we were working—stopping into businesses, being seen and stopping vehicles with violations. It's just that we got to enjoy the fall foliage, too.

I remember one year of this gorgeous ride in particular. With so many miles around the loop, it was difficult to believe we were in the right spot at the right time. It was mid-afternoon and Mickey and I had just driven through West Forks traveling south on Route 201. A call came over the radio that a small pickup had just sideswiped a Greyhound bus on Route 201 near Caratunk.

The pickup had stopped, then left the scene of the accident heading north. That meant the vehicle was coming right at us. The bus driver reported the operator of the vehicle was elderly and seemed confused.

The very next vehicle we met on Route 201 fit the description of the suspect vehicle. The whole driver's side of the small pickup was freshly damaged.

I flipped the cruiser around and, with blue lights on, stopped the vehicle. Sure enough, it was without a doubt the truck and person we needed to find. The vehicle was described perfectly, right down to where it would be damaged.

The driver was an elderly male, but his confusion was not due to being old or disoriented from the crash. Yup, you guessed it, he was snookered beyond reason. And from the moment I approached the operator, he had Mickey and I in stitches.

"What the hell do you want?" he bellowed at me when I approached the driver's door.

"Well Sir, do you know that you just had an accident back down the road a ways?" I asked him as I observed pieces of his vehicle dangling off the driver's side.

"He wouldn't get out of my way!" screeched the elderly driver.

"It was a Greyhound bus," I informed him.

"The bigger they are, the easier they fall," he replied, with a smirk on his face.

I was in total disbelief as I talked with this elderly gentleman. After getting his driver's license, I learned his name and that he was 83 years old. He was a distinguished-looking gentleman, tall and lean with white hair. He was very well spoken and he let me know right away that he was a native of West Forks and I was interfering with his Saturday ritual.

Which evidently meant that he got drunk Saturdays and drove to the market to get his groceries.

I told the suspect, whom we will call Mark, that we had to do an accident investigation and fill out some paperwork, and then I would have to process him for drunk driving.

"Drunk driving? What are you talking about? You should see me when I'm really drunk," he said. "I'm only a little drunk today!"

He continued, "I've been driving up here all these years without ever being stopped by the troopers and you're going to arrest me for drunk driving?"

"You give me no choice, Mark," I said. "I have to do my job and unfortunately for you, you got caught today."

"Damn old Greyhound buses!" he sputtered.

"Now Mark, I am going to make this as painless as possible for you," I said. "We can process you right here in the cruiser, get a blood alcohol test, and Mickey here will drive you home."

"What about my groceries?" he asked.

"Well, what about them?"

"I could use some help getting them into the house."

"We'll deal with that when we cross that path," I told him.

We processed Mark quite quickly. He was very jovial and kept cracking jokes through the whole ordeal. He sat in the back seat with the door open. He was a very nice guy, full of wit and making light of the whole situation. He also let us know if he wasn't too happy about something.

In other words, he got cranky pretty quick. One thing he got worked up about was the breath kit used to determine blood alcohol content. I took the contraption out of a sealed box, assembled it, and had him blow into it.

Mark kept looking at the contraption and looking at me and asking, "This thing does what?"

Some people had a difficult time blowing into the contraption. But after getting the complete history of the breath kit and how it worked, Mark blew it up and gave me a good sample.

Mark was completely processed and he wanted to know what we were going to do with him. I told him that he had been cooperative, even entertaining, and that we would get him and his vehicle home.

Mark just beamed knowing that he was going to be taken home and not all the way to Skowhegan to get locked up in jail. We made arrangements for Mickey to drive Mark's vehicle. Mark would ride with him to show him how to get him home.

I followed along. Within just a few miles Mickey drove the pickup into the dooryard of a beautiful old farmhouse on the bank of the Kennebec River. It had an attached barn and was very well kept. When I got out of my cruiser and approached Mark, all he could say was, "Grab an armful of groceries so I can get these into the house!"

I could not help but chuckle about the situation. It reminded me of an Andy Griffith show where Andy and Barney help citizens lug groceries into the house and make sure everything is OK before leaving. Mark was grateful and thanked us. He walked out onto the front porch to say goodbye as we left.

Mark settled into a comfortable rocking chair on the front porch and made wisecracks as we walked to the cruiser. Mickey told me what a nice guy Mark was and that he was going to go back and see if there was anything else we could do for him.

I told Mickey we had done enough and we should go. Mickey had other thoughts as he turned and went back on the porch to say goodbye one more time and to offer any other services.

Apparently, Mickey had overstepped his welcome. Just then I heard Mark screech, "I've been living in this house my whole life. I'm all set. Now get off my porch and leave me alone!"

I never saw Mickey run so fast to get in my cruiser and leave. I will never forget the image of the old man sitting in his rocking chair, rocking and cussing at us as we pulled away to finish our foliage ride.

Just another quiet day.

Revenge is Pungent

I would love to tell you about one of my skunk stories, which shall I say was 'explosive.'

When someone attempted retaliation toward law enforcement, it could only mean one thing — we were doing our jobs and apparently quite efficiently.

When someone plots revenge it shows the criminal element is thinking about cops and how to get them off their tails. I can tell you retaliation does not make law enforcement back off; it almost always brings more attention to the criminal.

As a young trooper in the Greenville area, I had finally caught someone who had never been caught before. I was told he was a career criminal committing mostly petty thefts.

I knew he wasn't really all that happy about being caught. From the moment I caught him with his 'hand in the cookie jar' he started to give me a hard time. I guess he thought striking back at me would make him feel better in some twisted way. Anyway, here is the story.

It took place in the late '70s in the summer in Greenville. Sometimes on my two days off, I headed south and visited my family or just got away from the area in which I worked.

I had just returned home in the evening and was slated to be on duty at 6 a.m. the following morning. The porch lights were on and as I walked across the porch I noticed little particles of mushy stuff stuck to the front side of my home. There must have been hundreds of little pieces. I could not figure out what it was, even upon close inspection. I shrugged it off as being some type of insect that flew into the side of the house and died. No big deal.

After I went inside and turned on the lights, my tenants came downstairs. Bill and Dawn were rather excited. "You wouldn't believe what happened here last night, Mark," Bill said.

"Uh, oh. What happened?" I asked.

"Just a little after midnight, I won't tell you what we were doing but there was a huge explosion out in front of the house. Followed by the most gagging smell," Bill said. "Just as soon as I could, I ran outside but didn't see anyone. But I was almost gagging on skunk smell, a hint of gunpowder and a little bit of smoke hovering over the front lawn."

I couldn't imagine what Bill was talking about. "What do you think happened?" I asked.

By then, Bill and Dawn were pretty calm since it had happened the previous night. "Someone blew a skunk up on your front lawn," laughed Bill. "Who have you ticked off lately, anyway?"

That made me put on my thinking cap. The problem was the list was quite long. Before going to bed, we went outside and examined the mushy pieces of stuff on the front of the house.

We saw that it was, indeed, bits of skunk. At least the odor was gone. Bill showed me the spot where the skunk was blown up on the front lawn. There was a little crater on the front lawn created by the gunpowder.

The following day, I could not wait to get to work to start to solve the mystery. You have to understand the area to be able to deal with the people. It was about woods and logging. The majority of the population was involved in the timber industry in one way or another, either by harvesting the trees, trucking them to a mill or running a sawmill.

One of the best tools that I had was a set of scales to weigh trucks that hauled the logs. If they were overweight the fines were hefty and could cut pretty hard into the profits that these guys worked so hard to make. No trucker liked to see the scales.

I narrowed the suspect field to a few people. Then I had to figure out who would know about it. I immediately thought of a trucker, John, who had ties to a few of the suspects that I had in mind.

I went to his house and noticed his tractor-trailer was fully loaded and parked on the side of the road. John usually trucked to Canada. To me it looked like the truck was very heavy. Rather than approach John at home, I waited for him to leave in the truck. I didn't have long to wait. Within a few hours, I met John driving north on Route 15 toward Canada.

I flipped around and made a traffic stop on John just north of Squaw Mountain. John got out and met me by the trailer.

I knew John quite well — well enough to never trust him. He hung around the criminal element and I knew he had a wealth of information. John smirked as I talked with him. I could tell right away that he knew what had happened on my lawn so I bluntly asked him what he knew.

Of course, he denied having any knowledge of any activity at my home, but his smirk worsened. So I leaned against his truck and started looking over the load.

"You know, John, this load looks pretty heavy."

John kept smirking, thinking I couldn't do a thing about his load as I was a road trooper and not a commercial vehicle trooper.

"You can't do anything about my load," he told me.

"I have something to show you, John," I said as I escorted him over to my cruiser. I reached inside and popped open the trunk. Then I brought John back to the open trunk which contained a set of scales.

"How do you like these?" I asked John as the blood drained from his face.

"Are you going to weigh me up?"

"Depends on how much you can tell me about that little incident on my front lawn," I told him.

It didn't take long for John to rat out the guy rather than pay a hefty fine for being overweight.

"It was Willy! He is so peeved at you for catching him last month. He found a dead skunk and couldn't think of a better place to put it than your front lawn. The thing is, though, he borrowed a quarter stick of dynamite and shoved it up the butt of the skunk, lit the fuse and threw it on your lawn from across the street, then ran as fast as he could before it ever blew up."

"Oh really!" was about all I could muster.

I cut John loose and started my search for Willy, a career criminal who never got caught before I arrived in town. Apparently I had been the first to catch old Willy and he didn't take to it very kindly. His crimes were mostly property crimes and everyone seemed to know that he was a thief, but he never got snagged.

I finally located Willy. Just as soon as I approached him the sweat started running down his forehead. Try as I might, though, I could not get him to admit to blowing up the skunk on my front lawn. I had to settle for knowing that I had him on another crime, and I hoped that justice would ultimately be served. That, and I made sure Willy knew that I knew he did it.

The funny thing about the whole incident was my tenants' night of "passion" had been rudely interrupted by the explosion and the mood was ruined by the skunk odor that permeated the house the rest of the night.

Oh well, just another quiet evening.

Rescue on Unity Pond

Every once in a great while, I got lucky and was in just the right place at the right time when a call came over the police radio.

Most of the time it seemed as though I had to travel across the county to respond to a call. But on this one particular day the planets must have been aligned and I was Johnny-on-the-spot as dispatch put out a call for assistance.

Headquarters was looking for a warden to respond to Unity Pond. A caller had told dispatch that he had observed a sailboat capsize in the lake and that its two occupants were having a hard time getting back onto the boat.

It was a beautiful, sunny, but cold late-fall day and a ferocious wind was blowing. Apparently these two people thought they would get in one last day of sailing before putting the boat away for the season.

The nearest warden was going to need better than an hour to get his boat and get to the lake. I lived within a quarter-mile of the lake and luckily I was patrolling in Unity at the time.

Being the owner of a 16-foot, high-powered ski boat, I volunteered to help. For once, I went through the proper channels to notify my immediate supervisor of what I was going to do.

My supervisor, Sgt. Mac Dow, cleared me to respond to the incident. This action saved my butt for what happened later ... but I'm getting ahead of myself.

The previous weekend I had cleaned my boat to get it ready for winter storage, but I had not yet parked it inside. I darted home, got my personal vehicle ready and hooked the boat up to it.

I was rushing ... that was my first mistake of the day. In my haste, I inadvertently had parked my cruiser in a bad spot behind the boat and forgot to move it. Yep, I did it. I backed the boat right into the side of the cruiser. I was barely moving when it happened but it dented the right front fender pretty good.

I told myself, "No time to worry about the little stuff now, just get to the lake." Which I did.

I drove to the Kanokolous boat landing and upon my arrival, a young volunteer firefighter, a fellow by the nickname of Teapot, was there.

He had heard the call on the scanner and was looking for the boat from the landing. I asked him if he wanted to go with me and give me a hand to help the people in distress. Teapot quickly said yes and helped me launch the boat. Off we went to locate the capsized vessel.

I have to describe the conditions of the lake that particular day. Like I said earlier, a gale was blowing, the waves were extremely high and rough, and we were in a low-lying ski boat — all the makings for another disaster. Let's just say I would have never taken my boat out on the lake that day for the fun of it.

Now, for my second mistake. When preparing the boat for winter storage, I had removed the drain plug. I didn't realize this until Teapot and I had traveled quite a distance out into Unity Pond. Water was pouring in as we were hitting the high spots of the waves and Teapot was hanging on for dear life with a very concerned look on his face.

I was quite sure he was thinking, "Why did I say yes to this madness!?"

Thank goodness I had placed the drain plug in the boat. As I slowed down a bit, I went to the rear of the boat and put it back in.

We quickly located the capsized sailboat — reaching it at the same time as other rescuers in another boat. We fished the people out of the water, tied their boat to ours and brought everyone to shore for a happy and safe ending to the ordeal.

After dropping the people at their camp on the Burnham shore, Teapot and I headed back to the landing to take my boat out of the water and call it a day. It was no easy task as the boat tossed this way and that in what seemed like Gilligan's three-hour tour.

We reached the landing and I don't think I ever saw Teapot move so fast. He jumped on shore, bent down on his knees and kissed the ground. I think his words were to the effect, "Don't ever ask me to get in a boat with you again."

Kind of brought a tear to my eyes.

I headed home to park the boat, get back in the cruiser and head to work when I saw the dent in the front fender and remembered that I had to contact my sergeant. I sheepishly phoned him to notify him of the incident. My sergeant, one of the greatest guys to ever wear a Maine State Police uniform, told me not to worry about it and to make the necessary arrangements to have it fixed.

End of story, right?

Well, not really.

I had the fender fixed and the bill was around $250. Troopers are self-insured, so it was going to come out of the budget. Months later I got a bill from the State of Maine for the $250.

To say the least, I was a little miffed and called the state official who had sent me the bill. I explained the situation to him and all he said was, "Too bad, fork over the money."

Well, that got my dander up even more. I told him flat out I was not paying for the damage, that it was done while on duty and the department was responsible for it. He told me that I was paying for it one way or another.

"We'll see about that," I screamed and hung up the phone. Thank goodness that I had followed protocol on that particular day and had gotten permission from my immediate supervisor.

My next phone call was to my good sergeant. As he always did, he told me, "Don't worry about it, Mark, I'll take care of it."

And take care of it he did. I never got another bill from that state official again. Thanks, Mac!

Just another quiet day on the high seas.

Just Five Minutes

State troopers sometimes do not know what kind of influence we had on children we're interacting with. We dealt with them in every aspect of life, including when giving talks at schools, Girl Scouts, Boy Scouts and bike rodeos.

What was especially hard, though, was dealing with domestic situations and seeing the fear in children's faces. I always made it a point to do my best to comfort the children in any way I could.

Perhaps the lowest I ever saw a child was after he saw his mom stab his father then attempt suicide. He must have wondered in all the confusion if he was to blame for what happened.

While his parents were recovering in the hospital, I did my best that night to make sure that child was in a safe place and with people who cared for him and loved him. Can you imagine what was going on in this child's head throughout that ordeal?

I did my best to leave a positive influence on all the children I dealt with in my career, mostly because of the interactions I had with troopers when I was younger and around my Dad. I got to meet some very well-known, big, tough troopers and every one of them left an impression on me. They also shaped my career aspirations.

Following are a couple of stories written by a couple of guys who were influenced by troopers when they were young.

* * *

This story is written by Trooper Tom Fiske, who remembers his first encounter with a Maine State trooper.

"I believe the children are our future. Teach them well and let them lead the way. Show them all the beauty they possess inside.

"Give them a sense of pride to make it easier. Let the children's laughter, remind us how we used to be."

OK, I know I totally just ripped off a Whitney Houston song just now, but it's true.

Where is he going with this you ask? My first experience with a Maine State trooper was 35 years ago when I was 6. I rode my bicycle right out in front of his cruiser as he was coming down the street.

Well, I was shaking in my $3 canvas Converse when I saw him stop and back up.

When he got out of the car, I'd have sworn he was 5-foot-40-inches tall with that Stetson hat on. Did I mention how scared I was? He knelt down, looked me in the face and asked my name.

I think I somehow managed to squeak it out. We had a brief conversation about bicycle safety before he got back into his car and drove off.

The fact that this encounter is as vibrant in my mind today as when it happened speaks volumes. It was less than five minutes of his time, but it affected me my whole life.

I know you are thinking, "Get on with it," but hang with me please. My parents taught me to respect authority and not just the police. I also learned to respect my elders.

The police officers in the small Maine town that I grew up in were heroes and people to be looked up to. I took comfort in knowing that they were always around.

When I became of age, I was lucky enough to be chosen to wear the uniform of a Maine State Police trooper. I'm still as proud today as I was those many, many years ago.

This morning, I was given one of those rare opportunities to positively influence a child. While I was finishing up at a crash scene, a man approached me with his 5-year-old son and explained that his boy loved police cars.

Well, I couldn't help but remember my own experience sooooooo many years ago.

Thanks to the wonder of modern technology, I was able to take this photo of young Zackary in the cockpit of a real Maine State Police trooper car and share it with you. Hopefully, the five minutes of my time will affect him in a positive way the rest of his life. Many thanks to retired Trooper Steve Pickering for having that bicycle safety chat with me so many years ago.

Zackary, age 5
Photo courtesy of Tr. Tom Fiske

Post Script: I'm about to let you into the inner sanctum of the mind of a police officer with this next bit of information. One thing that many parents do, without malice or ill intent, is to point to uniformed police officers and say, "You'd better behave or s/he will take you to jail."

When we hear this, it's like fingernails on a chalkboard. Please, we do not want your children to be afraid of us. We want them to be able to come to us when they need something. Instead, introduce the young lad or lass. We like talking to the wee ones. Semper Aequus.

--Trooper Tom Fiske, Maine State Police

* * *

The following story is written by Justin Faloon about his encounter with a Maine State Police trooper.

With all the negativity toward police officers around the country today, I'd like to share something positive. This is my fondest memory of the Maine State Police.

When I was quite young in the early 1970s, my father was the police chief of Howland. Howland is quite a small town by most standards these days, but in its day, it was quite different.

Although Howland was in its heyday, the police station was based in our home. Even the radio base station was in our house, which shows you how big the station was.

My mom would call my dad on the radio and tell him whatever she needed to and he would sometimes respond with, "I'm tied up right now."

Hearing that troubled me beyond belief. I imagined that some bad guy had my dad tied up. I'd put on my Western holster which contained my trusty Peacemaker and I had thoughts of "Backup is on its way." I guess my mom thought that he had it under control because she never let me go help.

Nothing made me happier than to jump in my dad's cruiser and ride with him. It reminded me of the "Andy Griffith" show. I'd always take my toy police car with me. It was an old black-and-white station wagon like the sergeant drove on "Adam-12."

You know, the one with the mobile command center and the tear gas gun in the back.

Justin Faloon sitting on his father's police car.
Photo courtesy of Tr. Tom Fiske

One time I was riding with him and we stopped so my dad could talk to a man and the man asked who the criminal was in the back. You want to talk about being slightly upset. I was no criminal, I was one of the good guys and I let him know what role that I played in the justice system. I'm not sure if my dad was smiling because it was funny or because he was proud, but I'd like to think proud.

One of my fondest memories was when my dad would meet a state trooper for coffee or lunch at what was then known as the A Frame Diner on Water Street in Howland. If I knew that he was meeting a trooper, I'd be sure to be with him. We always sat in the corner booth. I know it's hard to picture cops sitting at a corner table, right? I sat beside my dad staring at that trooper hat, wanting to put it on and be a Maine State Police trooper if only for a half hour or so. It was like a well-trained K9 told to stay with a T-bone steak loaded with gravy in front of him. He wants it badly, but he's too well trained not to dig in until given permission.

The part that made it so difficult was I had to ask to wear it. This sounds like an easy task, but I was a shy kid. I had to work up the courage and this took time, valuable time. Time was ticking and I wanted that trooper hat on my head. I finally summoned the courage and asked him to wear his trooper hat. He picked it up and handed it to me and I put that hat on and was a trooper for a whole coffee break. I wore that hat so proudly that I'd put a graduating cadet to shame.

I admired my dad for being a police officer and I'm proud of him as well. But being a Maine State Police trooper was my dream job. I never achieved that dream, but I'm not so sure that I'd do anything different with my career because all in all, I did some amazing things along the way.

One thing I wouldn't ever change is my support for the most professional, most honorable and most noble police agency in the United States.

The sad part of this story is I don't remember the trooper's name. My dad and mom have passed so I'm unable to share who it was. It doesn't make a huge difference I guess, as it's the memory that I cherish. Please remember you never know what might impact a child the most. Maybe it's the memory of being a Maine State trooper for a half-hour at a time.

Thank you Maine State Police. Stay safe and stay proud.

—Justin A. Faloon

As a side note to this story, after an investigation, it was learned the trooper who let Justin wear his Stetson and be a Maine State trooper was Trooper Brian Davis, who has since passed.

You never know when you might be able to influence a child...never let an opportunity slip by. It could change their life forever!

Did it Come From the Desert of Maine?

Motorists in Maine have more than 500 accidents a year involving moose. Civilians aren't the only ones who encounter moose in the road—occasionally a trooper does as well, with the same damaging results.

In the picture shown, the trooper was responding to a car/moose crash on I-95 in northern Maine.

This Maine State Police cruiser hit a moose in northern Maine.

On the way to the original crash, the trooper became a victim, striking another moose and destroying the cruiser. After severely denting the vehicle and crashing through the windshield, the moose wound up in the backseat of the cruiser. Luckily, the trooper in this incident walked away with minor injuries.

Moose often weigh more than 1,500 pounds and when hit broadside by a vehicle, their spindly legs give way and the large moose body often comes hurtling through the windshield with disastrous results.

Moose are most active in Maine in late spring and early summer. But trust me, if you live in Maine you can hit a moose any time of the year. Most Maine police officers have their own stash of moose stories and I want to share some stories that happened to other troopers.

This first story came from an elderly woman who attended a talk and book-signing that John Ford and I had and she wanted to share a story with us. She said that she and her late husband were very good friends with a Maine trooper who patrolled the northern part of the interstate above Bangor many years ago. The trooper had been called to a car/moose crash which involved an out-of-stater. This is what she told us:

An elderly gentleman from New York City was driving to Maine to visit relatives. Just outside of Bangor on I-95 he had an encounter with a large cow moose.

When most people think of a moose, they envision a bull moose with his stately rack of antlers. A cow moose, on the other hand, doesn't have antlers. She has small flappy ears, big rubbery lips, a hump on the back and long, spindly legs.

If this New York fella had hit a bull moose, maybe he would have thought he'd just had a bad encounter with one of Santa's reindeer. However, his front bumper hit the cow moose, took out her legs from under her, and she lay wounded in front of his vehicle.

When the trooper arrived at the scene, the frightened New York ran up to him, gasping, "Officer, quick! Call a vet! I've just hit a camel!"

Just in case you're wondering, there actually is a Desert of Maine and it's located outside of Freeport. But in all my years patrolling the roads of rural Maine, I have yet to see any camels trotting around.

* * *

Trooper Tom Fiske related this story to me one evening while telling stories about strange animals and excuses made by motorists.

He was called late one night to a tractor-trailer crash on I-95 north of Lincoln. The scene included a tractor-trailer hauling hazardous material that had gone off the interstate and was resting beyond the ditch on all its wheels. The driver very excitedly explained to the trooper that he veered off the road to avoid an elk. Really?! An elk?! There were no signs of any type of animal, including an elk, at the scene and the driver was arrested for OUI.

* * *

One of my first sergeants was originally assigned to Aroostook County. He too covered many crashes over his career. At the time of his assignment in The County, Loring Air Force Base was very active and lots of traffic flowed into the county from out of state. One of the car/moose crashes he covered involved airmen traveling from New York to Limestone.

They had struck a moose, causing it to come over the hood of the car and into the front passenger seat. The belly of the moose was ripped, and its stomach contents were seeping all over the inside of the car and all over the airmen. The paunch of any animal is as bad as it gets in the bad smell department.

When the trooper arrived, the airmen were outside of the totaled vehicle, desperately trying to get moose parts off their bodies and clothes. They had some real choice phrases coming out of their mouths as well.

When the trooper approached the airmen, one of them screamed, "Dam! You guys got really big rabbits up here!"

I told you, you just can't make this stuff up.

Maine's Biggest Manhunt

The following story is a fascinating tale about the shooting death of Maine Guide Wesley Porter of Patten, who was killed in 1943 in the North Woods near Webster Lake in Piscataquis County.

Following Wesley's death, an intensive nine-week manhunt commenced to find the killer. It ended in a shootout that fatally wounded Alphonse Maurence, a Canadian draft dodger.

I'd heard about this particular case for years, having read a bit about it in a book titled "Return of the Down East Detective," by Karen Lemke. When I was writing my columns, I came across the synopsis of the case in my dad's Maine State Police Academy notebooks.

It was fascinating reading. This case is truly a "whodunit" and illustrates in-depth investigative techniques and exceptional police work. It also depicts the dedication of several Maine law enforcement agencies, the Connecticut State Police and Maine citizens to track Porter's killer in some of the most dense and difficult terrain imaginable.

The troopers who investigated this case were true legends of the Maine State Police.

As I did more research on this case, I was astonished where it took me and who the principal players were. For instance, when I was a trooper patrolling in northern Piscataquis County, a nurse came to the Sheriff's Office to draw blood for many of the drunk drivers I removed from the highways.

I learned just a few years ago that she is the daughter of Maine Trooper James Mealey, the primary investigator of this murder case. I reconnected with the nurse, whose name is Jane Macomber. I visited with her and she allowed me to go through her father's Maine State Police materials. It was unbelievable to read his case file and notes and see photos of this murder.

I often mention Merle Cole, who was one of the original troopers in 1925. He was my neighbor in Vassalboro and a very good friend of my father. Other troopers involved in the case were Charles Marks and Lloyd Hoxie, who were brought in for their knowledge of the woods and tracking abilities.

Merle Cole (L) and Lloyd Hoxie (R)
Photo provided by Eric Albee.

This case also was written about in the 1940s in some detective magazines. You remember those, right? The ones that sensationalized stories and made it hard to believe what was written. Well, I was able to get my hands on at least three of the old magazines and found them to be factual and similar to police reports on the case.

Many people living in Maine in the summer 2015 will remember the massive manhunt that took place in the Guilford area of Piscataquis County. The suspect was wanted for murder in the shooting death of his ex-girlfriend.

The Wesley Porter manhunt took 66 days to complete in 1943. Seventy-two years later, the Guilford manhunt took 68 days to resolve; the suspect ultimately turned himself in. Thus, the Guilford manhunt recently became the longest manhunt in Maine history by two days.

There is a stark contrast between these cases, though. In my opinion, the suspect in the Guilford manhunt was helped and kept in a hiding place and was not on the run in the woods like Wesley Porter's killer in 1943.

I would like to relate one other oddity involving this case. I was speaking with an old friend and classmate, Eric Albee, who is the grandson of retired Lt. Merle Cole of the Maine Sate Police.

Eric told me his brother, Larry, dated a woman named Martha Alward. Larry introduced Martha to his parents, Phyllis and Lester, and during the conversation, Phyllis asked Martha about her grandparents. Martha said her grandfather was Wesley Porter, a Maine Guide from Patten who was killed in the North Woods by a man who had been breaking into camps.

Phyllis told Martha, "I have something to show you," and retrieved an old detective magazine that contained the story of Wesley Porter. There was a photo of Merle Cole on one page and a photo of Porter on the opposing page.

As fate would have it, today, Martha, the granddaughter of Wesley Porter, is married to Larry, the grandson of Lt. Merle Cole. This story has been full of similar coincidences.

This story is interesting for a number of reasons. The manhunt took longer than nine weeks and included every law enforcement agency in the state, as well as professional guides and many civilians. Even out-of-state law enforcement personnel assisted in the manhunt in northern Piscataquis and southern Aroostook counties. This case was solved by long hours of investigation, cooperation from different people who worked in the northern woods of Maine, and camp owners.

The camp owners were instrumental for a couple of reasons. They were able to provide what was stolen from their camps. This is one of the ways it was learned that the firearm used to kill Porter was a 20-gauge shotgun. They also found tattered clothing left behind and discovered clothes stolen from their camps. This gave a rough description of the height and weight of the killer. It also gave a description of what the killer would be wearing. The camp breaks even gave a timeline of where and when the killer was located in the woods and the direction in which he was traveling. From this information, law enforcement had a starting point to look for the killer of Wesley Porter.

Although this murder has been written about countless times, in chapters of books, in magazines, and newspapers, to do it real justice a book should be written about all the details of this case.

So, let's get to the story. The following is a summary of the Wesley Porter murder as found in the Maine State Police Academy notebooks of my dad when he went through the Academy in 1954 with a few corrections, additions, and new photos.

Wesley Morton Porter, 45 at the time of his death, was from Patten. He was married with eight children, was an excellent Maine Guide and was known to be a kind, nice and gentle man.

Wesley Porter
Photo provided by Martha Alward.

On May 31, 1943, Porter met three men who booked him to guide them during a week's fishing trip. They met in Sherman, took a taxi to Grand Lake Dam, and the following day went by boat to Second Matagamon Lake.

They left surplus supplies at a lumber office and hiked with backpacks into a camp on Webster Lake. These sportsmen were William Buchanan, 52; Robert Hames, 40; and Robert Jarvis, 26; all of Massachusetts. They spent the second day at camp getting everything settled and fishing in the vicinity.

The camp where Wesley Porter was murdered.
Photo provided by Jane Macomber.

Early the following day, Thursday, June 3, Porter went back to Second Matagamon Lake to pick up the surplus supplies and the party of men fished at Coffeelos Pond.

Porter returned about 5:30 p.m. and while he was preparing supper, he asked the men if they had fished at the dam. When they said they hadn't, Porter remarked that someone had been around that area.

Telos Dam
Photo provided by Jane Macomber.

After supper, Porter cleaned up and Jarvis reportedly went out on a steep ledge in front of the camp to watch for minnows for trout bait while the two older members of the party watched.

The men near the ledge heard a scratching sound behind the camp and Buchanan and Hames, both armed with .22 revolvers, circled in opposite directions, hoping to get a shot at what they thought might be a porcupine.

Suddenly, the stillness of the evening was shattered by a gunshot, followed a short time later by a second shot. Buchanan and Hames went toward the front of the camp and Jarvis huddled under the ledge.

When Buchanan got to the front of the camp, Porter was on the ground. His head was covered with blood and he was rolling back and forth.

"My God, Wes, what have you done?" Buchanan asked.

A third shot sounded and Buchanan and Hames thought Porter had been shot by a set gun—one that fires on an intruder or animal that trips a wire.

While Hames and Jarvis gave first aid to Porter, Buchanan used the camp phone to call the caretaker at Telos Dam, who relayed the call to Greenville.

Dr. F.J. Pritham, who also was the county medical examiner, arrived by plane at dark and found Porter mortally wounded—he died shortly after midnight, June 4, 1943.

The body of Wesley Porter on plane.
Photo provided by Jane Macomber.

At daybreak, Deputy Dave Knowlton of the Piscataquis County Sheriff's Office and Maine State Police Trooper James Mealey flew to the scene with Lt. Miller of the Civil Air Patrol. Their search revealed a 20-gauge shotgun shell, which had been exploded and a number of shots embedded in trees.

Tr. James Mealey and Dep. Dave Knowlton examining the tree.
Photo provided by Jane Macomber.

Dr. Pritham removed three similar shots from wounds in Porter's head during an autopsy in Greenville; these were sent to the State Bureau of Identification.

In the meantime, Deputy Chief Laurence C. Upton of the Maine State Police in Augusta ordered that a block be maintained at the Shin Pond outlet, the only way out of the area by boat or foot. Capt. Granville Seamans, commanding officer of the Maine State Police Barrack in Houlton, personally commanded this block.

Lt. Merle Cole, commanding officer of the area in which the shooting had taken place, flew to the scene in an Inland Fish and Game Department plane.

At his direction, Troopers Charles Marks and Lloyd Hoxie were flown in to search by boat the lake adjacent to the scene. They were looking for the 20-gauge shotgun, which the State Bureau of Identification had determined to be the death weapon.

The Piscataquis County Sheriff's Office and the Maine State Police assumed responsibility for the investigation, under the direction of the county attorney.

The Civil Air Patrol, State Forestry Department, Inland Fish and Game Department and guides offered their respective resources.

The three sportsmen were soon cleared of suspicion, as ballistics proved the fatal shot had not been fired by any of the guns they owned. A Massachusetts State Police investigation showed them to be of good moral character.

Other suspects, however, were numerous, including a nephew of the victim—a Greek-born trapper who had been convicted of poaching in New Hampshire—as well as a German man previously under investigation for subversive activities.

From information obtained and from particles of hair and clothing, authorities compiled a description of the wanted man. The description was given to all law-enforcement officials working on the case. It was later learned the facsimile bore a striking resemblance to the killer in terms of age, height and other characteristics.

Investigators rapidly became convinced the man for whom they were searching had been engaged in illegal hunting and trapping and/or in breaks of camps in that area. Many break-ins had occurred during that winter, and 20-gauge shotgun shells and shotguns had been stolen from two of the camps. Other breaks were investigated as they were reported, and the path of the thief, and possible killer, seemed to be heading north.

At a break-in at a camp on Chamberlain Lake, a 20-gauge shell was found and ballistics showed it to be identical with that found at the scene of the murder.

Clothing was seized from a camp and the State Bureau of Identification drew a description of the wanted man. Again, an updated description of the man was forwarded to all area law-enforcement officers, guides and hunters.

July 31, Warden Bert Duty was spending the night in a warden camp on Soper Mountain. During the night, a shot was fired into the camp. The warden returned fire, but missed. The shell that Warden Duty found turned out to be identical with the other two from the shooting scene.

Wardens, foresters, deputy sheriffs, guides and Maine State Police officers peppered the area and watched the trails around the clock. Warden Supervisor Helon Taylor and Warden Duty found the suspect's makeshift lean-to, but he had left and was apparently living in the swampland.

Lt. Cole wanted bloodhounds and, with the permission of Maine Gov. Sumner Sewall, a request for K-9s was sent to Commissioner Edward Hickey of the Connecticut State Police. Hickey obliged and sent two top bloodhounds and their handlers, Troopers Adam Beaudry and Emil Struzik.

They were flown aboard an Inland Fish and Game Department plane to the scene and went to work August 7. That night the dogs picked up a scent. Due to the difficulties of traveling at night in the swamp, they stopped the track at about 9 p.m. The dogs, though, had already done their work.

At dawn, Albert C. "Chub" Foster, a close friend of Wesley Porter, and Clinton Porter, the son of the victim, were hiding in the brush watching the trail leading from Fourth Musquacook Lake to Third Musquacook Lake.

They heard a noise and saw a man fitting the description of the suspect coming from Clear Lake Mountain. He was carrying a pack, an ax and a shotgun.

When the stranger was about 20 feet away, Foster said, "Just a minute, Mister."

The man reportedly dropped his ax and started to raise his shotgun. Foster shot first, hitting the man between the hip and knee of his right leg. No bones were reportedly broken and first aid was provided.

Soon Lt. Cole arrived and took custody of the man. The man couldn't speak English so Lt. Cole questioned him with the help of a French interpreter.

The man identified himself as Alphonse Maurence, 35, single, of Quebec. He had several aliases. He said he had been in the woods for three years total and in the Maine woods for one. He said he left Canada because he didn't want to be drafted into the army.

Maurence said he broke into camps for food and clothes, and that he had taken a shotgun and shells from one of them. Maurence said he fired into camps to make certain no one was there and said during the summer he approached a camp where he saw two men standing. He claimed he shot over their heads to frighten them away so he could get something to eat.

Maurence died August 8, after being flown to the Greenville hospital, 12 hours after being shot on the trail—which he said he took because he thought he could go faster and get away from the dogs.

Thus ended what until 2015 was the biggest manhunt in Maine.

Boys Will Be Boys

When patrolling as a trooper, one thing was for sure, I never knew what was going to happen next!

I am still not sure how I would react if my son ever did what the boy in this particular story did, especially due to my love of older, special-interest autos.

It started late one evening in early summer when I was called to a motor vehicle crash on the Hall-Dale Road in Montville. Rescue also was en route, as it had been reported the driver was injured.

I arrived on scene just after rescue; the operator was already in the ambulance. I observed an antique auto wrapped around a tree. I made mental notes to myself about it as I made my way to the ambulance to check on the operator. It appeared to be a vehicle from the 1950s — a station wagon, very, very nice condition and something I had never seen before. And by the damage it had suffered, it looked like I would never see it on the road again.

The ambulance crew was working on a boy about 15 years of age. His injuries were not life-threatening. He mostly had bumps, scrapes, cuts and bruises that needed attention and then he would be taken to the hospital in Belfast.

It did not take long to realize the operator was clearly under the influence of alcohol and had no license. All of this was getting to be confusing. Why and how was a 15-year-old boy driving around drunk in an antique auto with no license?

He had some serious explaining to do. The ambulance was getting ready to depart for the hospital, so I told its personnel that I would meet them at Waldo County General Hospital as soon as I cleared the crash scene.

The antique auto was being driven in a southerly direction and simply did not make it through a normal curve in the road. It appeared as though the driver was simply going too fast for the curve and slammed on his brakes when he realized he was not going to make it through the curve. We all know what happens when you lock up your brakes.

Yep, you go straight ahead. Which is what the antique did, straight ahead into a tree.

The vehicle was completely demolished. This saddened me as I could tell someone had put a lot of work into it and it was probably the owner's pride and joy. After cleaning up the scene and having the antique auto removed and returned to the owner's home, I headed to the hospital to deal with the driver.

I requested the boy tell me the whole story. Seems as though his mom and dad had gone to visit relatives in another state and had left their son home alone for a few days.

The teen son, feeling a sense of independence, made the most of it. The first thing he did was get into the cabinet where his dad kept the liquor. After getting a whole lot of liquid courage, he decided to take his father's antique auto for a little spin.

It was late and dark, and he thought no one would be the wiser or see him drive the vehicle. Especially since he didn't even have a license. So off he went. And then, disaster. He wrecked his father's beautiful car.

The parents had to be notified. I realized a long time ago it is very important for parents to hear their child's voice first.

That way they would know she or he was alive, if not well. I dialed the number where the parents were staying and handed the phone to the boy. I told him that he needed to let them know that he was OK, and that someone else needed to speak with them.

"Dad? I've had a little accident," he told his father. There was a long pause and then he said, "Just talk with the police, as they need to speak with you anyway." And the son handed over the phone to me.

"Sir? This is Trooper Nickerson with the State Police. I need to speak with you concerning your son being involved in an accident tonight," I told him.

"Is he OK?"

"He's a little banged up but he is going to be OK," I told him.

"Who was he with?" the father inquired.

"He was alone," I said.

"What do you mean he was alone? He has no license. Whose vehicle was he driving?" the father asked.

"Well, he was driving your antique station wagon," I explained.

"He was driving *what*?"

"Your antique station wagon," I again told him.

There was dead silence.

"You say he is OK though, right?" he again asked.

"Yes, he is going to be fine, but there is more," I told the father.

"What more could you possibly tell me?" the father inquired.

"Well, he's drunk."

"He's *what*?"

"He's drunk."

"Well, where did he get that?" the father asked.

"From your liquor cabinet, is what he told me," I replied.

"You do what you need to and his mom and I are on our way home," he said as he hung up.

I hung up the phone and looked at the boy. His head was hanging low and he was staring at the floor. "I'm in big trouble, aren't I?"

"Yes, you are. More so with your dad than you ever are with the law," I told the son.

After I took care of the paperwork and after the boy was treated, he was allowed to go home with a relative.

I always wanted to be a fly on the wall when his father got home to deal with him. One thing I can say though, is that I never had another dealing with that boy throughout his teen years.

Just another quiet evening in Waldo County...except for probably at the boy's house.

"My Pocketbook Was Stolen"

You'll read in the story of 'Legendary Trooper Dave Giroux' the wonderful training I received from this oversized trooper. He taught us well and saved many troopers from ever getting injured while on patrol dealing with violent offenders. One part of the training was doing a sprint of 100 yards plus or so while racing another trooper cadet, then getting into the wrestling position and wrestling each other until one of us was pinned. It taught me a lot about 'it ain't over 'til it's over,' meaning you still have to handcuff someone after you catch them. This particular training came in very handy in a short period of time after I started patrolling the roads of Maine.

It wasn't even a year before I got to use this technique. I was flagged down by a frantic lady while driving through Waterville on Main Street one day. I pulled over and she yelled that some guy had just stolen her pocketbook. He was with some other guys behind a gas station in the intersection.

I told her to follow me and point out who did it. We walked around the corner of the building and saw five guys in a circle. At that point, I did not need her help anymore. One of the men still had the pocketbook in his hand.

These guys never saw me and my intention was to quietly walk up and grab the guy with the pocketbook and arrest him.

It was not to be. My victim was overly anxious and yelled, "It's the guy with my purse!" She yelled so loud that they turned, saw my uniform and ran off in different directions. I took off after the guy with the pocketbook.

I was quite young then, just a year removed from the academy and still in pretty good physical condition. So I could still run fairly fast, even with all the equipment around my gun belt. I followed the suspect around the back of the garage, to College Avenue, up the sidewalk, and in and around many parked cars.

I was gaining on him and thought for sure that I would soon have him in my grasp. Then he ran across the street and around another parked car. I saw an opportunity that if I could jump over the hood of the parked car, I would land right on him.

I saw it in the movies all the time right? Well why not me?

So I jumped to get over the hood of the car. Not so! My heel caught the far end of the fender and I went sprawling belly down on the sidewalk on the other side, just missing my prey as I fell to the pavement.

I quickly got up and continued chasing my suspect. I think he thought that he had lost me. He went into a private yard and climbed under some rose bushes, trying to hide. I ran up to him, saw him on all fours under the bushes, breathing like a racehorse after a long race. I, too, was quite winded and was glad the chase was over. Then my training kicked in and I remembered it wasn't over until I had him handcuffed.

I put my right hand on his neck and told him it was over and to come out. He did not move. I again gave him a warning to come out and give up. He tried bolting, but thankfully I had a good grip on his neck and when he attempted to get away, we both tumbled on the lawn and the wrestling match was on. I was able to get one handcuff on and hold him down but that other handcuff just wasn't making it around his other wrist.

Without realizing it, our actions had apparently caught the attention of quite a few bystanders. While I was on top of my suspect and inches from getting that other handcuff on, a middle-age man came over to assist me.

"The law may keep this trooper from hurting you but it doesn't keep me from helping the trooper," he told my suspect. With that, the Good Samaritan put one foot on my suspect's throat and kept pressing until he gave up. I was then able to get the second handcuff on and the fight was over. Or so I thought.

I told my Good Samaritan, "Thank you. I'm not even going to look up at you so you can't be identified."

Just then, the Waterville police showed up and I was quite exuberant. I finally felt safe, as I didn't know whether or not this suspect's buddies might have followed us. I would have been in a real jam without further help.

The officer getting out of the cruiser was none other than "Big Jim." He called my suspect by name and scolded him. He opened the rear door of his cruiser so that he could put my suspect into the cage.

Well, "Big Jim" came over, grabbed my suspect with one hand and literally threw my suspect toward the open door of the cruiser. However, he missed, not once but twice before he got the bad guy stuffed into the cruiser. And then they were gone. I was still sitting on the lawn watching all of this. I thought to myself, I guess that's the way they do it in the city.

I quietly went to the police station, retrieved my handcuffs and hurried back to the North Country, thanking Dave Giroux for that wonderful training.

Just another day on patrol.

Caught Off Guard

During my career, I learned that everyone was different and reacted differently in similar situations. I just never knew what might happen, and I learned not to stereotype people. I learned this the hard way.

As I have written before in some of my stories, over the course of my career I removed a lot of drunk drivers from our highways; I processed more than 1,300 people for operating under the influence.

For the most part, I was able to read them and fend off action that might put me or someone else in danger. No one likes to have their freedom taken away and be put into a situation where they might be going to jail.

I always believed that as long as I was firm and fair, people would understand that I had no choice in the matter and that we should get through the process as quickly and painlessly as possible.

I rarely had fights with people I arrested for OUI, although there were a few. Let's face it, some people just did not want to go to jail.

But I had a weakness. It took me a long time to keep up my guard with older women who reminded me of my mother. I just could not believe I was catching people for OUI who looked like my mother. Thankfully, that did not happen very often.

When my guard was down, something embarrassing always happened. Older ladies frequently lectured me that I should be letting them go.

"How can you do this to a lady such as I?" I would get asked.

And when I continued with the OUI process, I would get scolded. Once I even got slapped in the face. But I took it as my fault for not paying closer attention.

I thought I would share one of these situations. This, though, did not involve an older woman, but a very short, thin, young man who might have weighed 90 pounds soaking wet.

I made the traffic stop on Route 15 just south of Monson. It was well after midnight, and I had a rider along with me. The rider's name was Lindsay and he was great company. Lindsay was a good friend and had part-time law enforcement experience. He was also a good-sized guy and quite capable, as he was a football player during his high school days. We always found lots to do, and the night went by quickly with much laughing.

I approached the operator after stopping the weaving vehicle. The young man was all alone and it was clear right from the beginning that he was snookered, what we call a "keepah!"

I had the young man come back to my cruiser so I could speak with him. Once he was inside, I asked him questions about his activities that night.

He admitted to drinking quite a bit at the Wagon Wheel and he was headed home since the bar closed. Lindsay was in the backseat behind the OUI suspect, half-listening to the conversation as I put the suspect through the process.

It was clear after he admitted how much he had consumed that I would be giving him a breath test to determine his blood-alcohol content. He seemed very calm and cooperative. He was a nice guy who made a bad decision to get behind the wheel after drinking too much.

Even if he had become violent, I don't think he could have fought his way out of a wet paper bag, he was so little.

When offering a blood alcohol test, it is state law to read the implied consent form. To be honest, I thought the form was very confusing, even to a sober person, never mind all the drunks I had to read it to. No doubt a lawyer penned it.

When reading it to the OUI suspect, I explained what each paragraph meant and then moved on when the suspect acknowledged understanding.

While reading this form, and getting a nod of comprehension, I looked back down to read the next paragraph. All of sudden my head bounced off the side glass of my cruiser window. I was dazed for a second or two before I realized my little OUI suspect had spun around in his seat and kicked me in the head while I was reading that foolish form.

As I gathered my senses, I grabbed his ankle and started subduing the little guy. But I could not get a good grasp to pull him toward me so I could smother him and handcuff him.

I kept reaching for his neck but couldn't find it as he was flailing both feet at me. I finally figured out why he would not come toward me. Apparently, after the first kick at my head, Lindsay reached from the back seat and got the OUI suspect in one swipe. He hooked him around his neck and pulled him between the seat and the door frame.

Both Lindsay and I were pulling on him in unison, almost ripping him apart in the middle. The little guy was completely wedged in by the door frame and could not move. I had to go outside the cruiser, around to the passenger side, open the door and pull the little guy out from between the seat and the door frame.

"Now why in the world did you kick me in the head?" I asked him.

"Felt like it," he told me.

The little guy got handcuffed and lugged off to the county lockup. That was the last time I let my guard down with a small guy. And I never got kicked in the head again while reading that foolish form.

Just another quiet night in the life.

Bringing in the New Year

Writing these stories has been a lot of fun. I get to relive my career all over again and get in touch with people I dealt with throughout my time as a trooper.

And one cannot forget that I get to pick on my old friend, retired Warden John Ford. I have received e-mails from as far as Australia and England and many from people in the United States.

Many old friends have written, as well as relatives from all over, people who recognize themselves in the stories and others who thank me for telling it like it was.

Recently, I was contacted by a woman who had come across my articles on *VillageSoup*. She remembered me from when she had a scrape with the law. It was fun communicating with her about her life since then and about all the twists and turns life has to offer. I warned her that I might have to tell her story someday as well. So here goes.

It was New Year's Eve 1988. I had worked most New Year's Eve nights since I had become a trooper some 11 years earlier. I had learned that right about midnight the roads were basically empty.

People were either asleep or, for the most part, were at a party celebrating. From past experience, I thought I would have a good hour or so before traffic picked up. This would give me time to rush home and celebrate the stroke of midnight with my family, tuck them into bed and head off on patrol.

On this particular New Year's Eve, I was at home celebrating when I got the call from State Police Headquarters of a motor-vehicle crash on the Weeks Mills road in South China. It was just barely after the stroke of midnight as I drove to the scene of the crash.

I remember wondering why a person would be out right at midnight. It was a single-vehicle crash, wherein the car had slid off the road and into the ditch. The driver was slightly injured and had to be transported to the hospital. I observed her briefly before the ambulance drove away. It was obvious I was going to have to charge her with drunk driving. I cleaned up the scene, got the car towed, then headed to the hospital to deal with the operator.

In the emergency room, I located the accident victim, who was in her early 20s and dressed for partying on New Year's Eve. The problem was she had way too much to drink to be driving. I'm not sure if she thought she was going to be able to talk her way out of her problem, but I certainly thought she was trying her hardest.

As I listened to her story and gathered what information I needed for the investigation, her demeanor started to change. She became very groggy and put her head down on the emergency room bed.

I started to explain the issue of her drinking and driving and advised her that I would be charging her with operating under the influence of alcohol. She suddenly opened her eyes, looked right at me, turned her head toward me and puked. Ugh!

It ran down the front of my uniform and landed on my shoes. I don't do well when things like that happen; I gag as well. Thankfully, she had a lot to drink that night instead of a lot to eat.

Over and over she apologized. I was thankful not to be puking right along with her. A blood sample was taken and I wrote a summons for her to appear in court. I knew I had to get out of the ER as soon as I could or I would have ended up sick. And that is how I spent New Year's Eve 1988.

Just another quiet evening in the life of a trooper.

Patty and Her Bicycle

In my books, I try to write about the lighter, funnier side of police work. There are a lot of hilarious happenings in the life of a trooper, but there are some extremely sad ones as well. In my last book, I wrote about the difficulty I had doing death notifications—when I had to notify a mother that her young son's life had been taken by a drunk driver, I hugged her and cried right along with her. Death notifications are one of the saddest and hardest aspects of police work. We were given extensive training at the Maine State Police Academy on how to perform death notifications, as the Academy hired role models to act as grieving survivors, to teach law enforcement officers how to best deal with the extreme emotions involved in a death. We were taught that each person needs to grieve in their own particular way. Some people scream and cry, some people's faces sort of cave in and the light goes out of their eyes, while others are numb and speechless with shock before the tears start. However they react, it's never easy to break bad news to loved ones.

I'm going to warn you right now, this is not a funny story in any way, as it involves the violent deaths of children. If you are squeamish or emotional, you may find this as hard to read as it is for me to write, and you may be better off moving along to the next chapter to find something a bit easier on your heart and mind.

Unfortunately our job was to deal with many tragedies in life and this was certainly one for me. Before I had my son, this type of thing didn't bother me nearly as much. I went to a scene, dealt with what I had to, broke bad or sad news to loved ones and tried to not let it bother me, before moving on to the next incident.

But these were different for me. I was called to Searsport to assist the Sheriff's Office to reconstruct a fatal motor vehicle crash. The Maine State Police are usually called by the local jurisdictions to assist in a fatality investigation. When I got to the scene, I was briefed on the details as they were known to the deputy sheriff. This accident happened in front of a church. The details are this....a young mom's job was to clean the church. She brought her five-year-old daughter with her while she did this job. The little girl, we'll call her Patty to give her a name for this story, had just learned how to ride a bicycle. The mom thought that the church parking lot would be a good place for her to practice riding her bike. So the mom got Patty's new red bicycle out of the trunk of her car and let Patty start riding the bike around in the parking lot. The mom had gone into the church to start her cleaning job. In your mind's eye I'm sure you can see this little blonde child, an innocent little girl, just riding her bike on a warm summer day.

Now the layout of the parking lot was level up by the church, but the driveway leading up to it was on a slight uphill incline. While Patty was riding around the parking lot she decided to go down the driveway and got going too fast. Patty was not able to or experienced enough to know how to stop the bike, which required her to back-pedal to brake and stop, and she started rolling downhill too fast. Unable to stop the bike, she was heading straight for the road and directly in the path of a large dump truck. The driver of the dump truck, seeing the little blonde girl freewheeling down the church driveway and realizing the danger, did all he could to stop his dump truck. But he couldn't get it stopped. From the skid marks left at the scene, he must have stood on the brakes. The little girl went directly in front of the dump truck and was struck and killed, eventually landing on the shoulder of the road.

Although little Patty was removed from the scene by medical personnel, it was still a gruesome sight upon my arrival. With a mangled red bike, her blood splattered and pooled on the shoulder of the road and a long set of brake marks left by the dump truck, it was for me to decipher and try to learn if the dump truck was going too fast or was legally within the law. But I have to tell you, having a son about the same age as Patty, it was really bothering me thinking about this little girl's last moments on this earth. I saw something on Facebook not too long ago that reminded me of this case, it was a post someone had made, with the arms of a child reaching up, and the inscription said, "The most gorgeous jewels you'll ever own are the arms of your child around your neck." How true. We don't always fully realize how small and precious and fragile children actually are until you encounter a tragedy like this.

While I was working on the accident reconstruction, which involves a considerable amount of math and measurements to calculate vehicle speed, velocity and braking maneuvers, Patty's father came to the scene of her accident. It has always been my belief to let people grieve in only the way people can. This poor Dad got out of his car, went to the shoulder of the road where Patty's blood was pooled, got down on his knees and started to rub the bloody gravel all over his face and arms, his chest heaving with deep heavy sobs. I wanted to protect him from being hit by passing motorists, but I felt the need to let him grieve, in his time, in his way. I could only imagine his thoughts and feelings, losing this beautiful little girl, and he'd never get the chance to see her go to school, celebrate her next birthday, or see what she could have blossomed into in her life. I eventually helped the Dad to his feet and got him back to his car. With my hand on his shoulder, it was a short walk, but long on thoughts. Believe me, it was a difficult walk for both of us.

The investigation determined the dump truck driver did nothing wrong. However, I'm sure that poor driver had a lot of sleepless nights, tossing and turning with his own "if only" thoughts. It was just a terrible, terrible accident that was no one's fault, and if it had just happened a minute earlier or a minute later, Patty would still be alive today. I remember when I left the scene, I went straight to my home, found my son and gave him a big hug and a squeeze. I spent quite a bit longer tucking him in that night, and maybe he got an extra bedtime story. I know I spent more time with him in the days after Patty.

The Maine State Police try to take a very active role in community outreach and education. We offer Bicycle Safety Programs and encourage young riders to wear helmets, and to learn to ride their bike properly and safely. See the attached picture of Trooper Herman Boudreau handing out bike safety leaflets, way back in 1959. Incidentally, the little feller in the baseball hat shooting a big grin at Trooper Boudreau is about the size of Patty in this story.

Photo courtesy Tr. Tom Fiske

The other incident I want to convey to you involved a neighbor of mine who lived only a few houses down the road from me. He was a 14-year-old boy who was killed in a motor vehicle crash while riding with his friends. We'll call him Billy just to give him a name in this story.

I knew Billy quite well. I used to see him riding his bike all the time in the neighborhood. He was friendly and was always asking me questions about being a trooper and how much I liked my career. He would come to our dairy bar and have an occasional ice cream. I always liked the boy.

Well, Billy had a couple of friends, and one of them had a girlfriend who had just gotten her license. It was a beautiful sunny day when I got a call to respond to a motor vehicle crash on the Whitaker Road in Troy. Before my arrival, I was notified that it had turned fatal.

Upon my arrival, I observed a mid-size car off the left side of the road and against a tree stump. The vehicle had come to a sudden and abrupt stop after leaving the travel portion of the road. On the ground lying beside the vehicle was a young boy. There were two other teens standing near him. I went over to them and immediately recognized the young boy as Billy. There was not a mark on him except for a little blood coming from one of his ears. I checked for signs of life, there were none. Billy was dead. I couldn't believe it.

The other teens told me after they crashed that everyone got out and were walking around. Everything seemed fine. Then all of a sudden, Billy just dropped to the ground and they couldn't get him to talk. He stopped breathing.

But the hardest part was the arrival of his Dad. A person I knew well. He came running to Billy, got down on his knees, grabbed his son and hugged him. And kept hugging him, wailing for him to wake up. I was not going to stop him. I let the Dad do what he needed and after a period, started to persuade him to let go of his son. Finally he did, and I escorted him back to his family and into his car. I told him I would take care of everything at the scene and see him later to advise him of anything he wanted to know.

These cases were hard and even harder to forget. As a matter of fact, I'll never forget them.

Dope Growers

During my career, I picked, plucked, chopped, cut and carried out of the woods more marijuana than entire villages could smoke in a generation.

Most of the time, a person or persons got charged with cultivating or possession, and sometimes the illegal plants were picked and destroyed.

It was a cat-and-mouse game figuring out who was growing the pot and then trying to catch them. Eighty percent of the time it wasn't that hard to figure out the grower's ID due to where the plants were located.

Sometimes we could follow a direct, well-worn path from a residence to the plants. Based on that evidence, a search warrant would be obtained, especially if the plants were within the curtilage of the home.

Other times, we had to guess who the grower was. If I could not figure it out, I opted to have a little fun.

If the plants were in Monroe, I would pick the name of a townsperson whom I suspected grew the pot and leave a note using that person's first name.

It would read something like: "Got your plants. Thanks a lot, Dave." And I would attach it to one of the cut-down marijuana stalks.

At times, I could figure out who owned plants in the woods, but it was necessary to catch him or her tending the plants to prove ownership in the court.

This took surveillance and time, which were not luxuries of the job. So, I used the believed-to-be grower's name and another dope grower's name as the person who took them.

That note might read: "Hey Steve, really appreciate the hard work you did on these plants. Thanks a lot, George."

It was interesting to see what type of reaction the notes would evoke. You would not believe the tips the grower would give up about the other person.

Of course, I never received any complaints of theft from any of these growers. I wonder why.

Sometimes, I got calls and visits from delivery drivers. They would tell me about suspicious activity at various homes and I would follow up with an investigation and, sometimes, arrests.

One day, though, when I was at an accident scene and was going to be busy for a while, a delivery truck driver stopped and told me about marijuana plants he just observed while making a delivery.

He told me exactly where I could find them in the person's garden and that they were tied down because they had grown faster and taller than all the vegetables.

I knew I would not be able to get to this matter for a few days the legal way, which meant the information would become stale.

So, I did it the quick way. After clearing the accident scene, on my way to the hospital to check on the victims, I stopped at the residence, went straight to the garden and picked the marijuana plants.

I threw them in my trunk, took out a Maine State Police business card and left it on the front door. It read: "I have your plants. If you would like to talk with me, call me at the following number. Trooper Nickerson."

I never did get a call from them. Can't understand why.

This leads to a story about a marijuana patch in the area of Brooks/Jackson. I only am able to tell my side of this story, as I was dragged into this by my old friend, Warden John Ford.

But here is my version:

John had received information about some illegal plants and after checking it out he found a marijuana patch in the woods near a particular home.

John determined the probable owner was a businessperson in the Brooks area. John looked over the stuff pretty well—it was well maintained and yielding a huge crop. It was worth dedicating time with this patch to see if we could catch the person with the plants.

There was not enough time to do surveillance, so John and I thought we might push things to make them happen sooner rather than later. We hatched a plan of action to catch the person in the patch.

After hatching the plan, John and Deputy Warden Scott Sienkiewicz drove to the area, hid the warden truck and situated themselves among the plants.

I went to John's house in Brooks and made a phone call. Thank goodness there was no such thing back then as Caller ID. I told the suspect, "Hey Al, the cops are on their way to pick your dope!"

I hung up the phone and went to my cruiser. The warden plane was flying overhead to observe the suspect's movements in the event he took the bait.

Sure enough, he did. As I got back into the cruiser, Warden Pilot Dana Toothaker radioed that the suspect had just left his store and got into his van.

The suspect was on a dead run. Dana followed the van from Brooks Village to the suspect's residence.

After the suspect ran in to his house, he quickly came back outside, went into a shed and emerged with a chainsaw. He loaded the chainsaw into the van, drove to the little woods road that led to the illegal plants, parked and cut down a couple of trees to block the access road.

Dana observed the suspect walk into the woods toward John and his warden deputy and Dana warned them the guy was on his way in.

In the meantime, I had driven to a location not far from where John and Scott were hiding and I waited.

And waited. And waited. I am a very impatient person. But the wait was worth it.

After it was over this is what John explained to me about the happenings in the marijuana patch.

John and Scott had taken up a hiding position so they could observe any activity in the patch. They watched Al come into the patch and look at the plants. They wanted to see Al actually touch the plants to make a better case. It was a long wait for him to do that but finally he went over to one plant and touched it.

That is when John confronted the suspect and told him he was under arrest. The suspect had a machete and was raising it up during the confrontation. That is when Scott stepped out and racked a round into the 12-gauge shotgun he was carrying.

The confrontation ended abruptly, Al was taken down and a .32 caliber semi-automatic handgun was taken out of the waist of Al's pants.

The suspect was charged with trafficking and taken to Waldo County Jail. A pickup truck load of marijuana was confiscated and taken to the evidence locker in Belfast.

We took some marijuana and had it analyzed by the lab. The conclusion—it was perhaps the best they had seen in this state. The suspect had spent a lot of time grafting and filling in the stalk. The crop had been well fertilized and each plant was moist and potent.

At the trial, the suspect was found guilty and sentenced to a short few days in the county lockup. After the trial, the clerk of courts who recorded the evidence told us, "Oh my God, you guys are sneaky!"

Just another quiet day in Waldo County.

Luckiest Kid I Ever Met

One important duty of a Maine State Police trooper is to investigate motor-vehicle crashes. Each year, I investigated hundreds of them and I can tell you that no two of them are the same.

I got my very first surprise when I patrolled the northern woods of Piscataquis County. I arrived at a two-vehicle collision on Route 16 in Sebec that had been called in as an unknown personal injury accident.

I was flabbergasted at what I saw—two full-size pickups were literally torn apart in the middle of the road. I thought no one could have lived through such a violent crash. No one was inside either vehicle. An onlooker said the drivers were at a nearby store.

There, I met with two perfectly calm people drinking coffee who said they were the operators. Inexplicably, neither one of them had a scratch.

Another evening, I arrived at what appeared to be a minor accident—a vehicle had gone off the road and struck a small tree. There seemed to be minor damage to the vehicle. When I got to the car, I saw the seat-belted operator was deceased.

Now why in the world did this person die in a minor crash but two people walked away from a major head-on collision in which the vehicles were literally torn apart? Some things just do not make sense.

I saw this type of thing over and over throughout my career. My thought was that God decides who goes and who stays.

One late spring/early summer night, there was fog thicker than I'd ever seen before. I literally could not see more than a few feet in front of my cruiser. Basically, it was not safe to be on the road. It was getting late and conditions were getting worse, if that was possible. I dared not to travel more than 10-15 mph as I responded to calls.

Then I got a call I had been dreading—a motor-vehicle crash on Route 9 in South China. Fortunately, I was close by. When I came upon the scene, I was shocked and angered at what I saw.

A tractor-trailer truck driver had decided to park his rig in a large parking lot and rather than drive forward into the lot, he had backed across the street and into the lot. That put his rig all the way across the road and that, in turn, blocked the street completely. And with visibility being nil...

The driver tried to get the rig backed into the lot before any other traffic came but that did not happen.

I walked around the rig that still stretched all the way across the road and saw a vehicle that had crashed into the trailer.

It was just like at the movies. The vehicle had literally gone under the trailer; its windshield was the first part of it that made contact with the rig. The vehicle did not stop until the front half of the roof had been ripped off; the driver's seat being under the trailer.

I thought for sure the driver would be dead. I looked in the rear window and saw a teenage boy lying in the seat. His eyes were open and he appeared to be OK. I couldn't believe my eyes.

He made his way out of the car through a rear door; all he had for injuries were some minor cuts from all the flying glass. I kept asking him if he was OK and he said that he was fine.

The youth said he had been driving along the road and was having difficulty seeing in all the fog. All of a sudden, he saw something across the road but couldn't tell what it was. His only choice was to slam on the brakes and try to stop. Having only feet in which to stop, it was not possible. This, for me, is where God comes in. The driver said he stood on the brake and braced himself and when he did, the back of the seat broke and he went over backwards, thereby saving his life.

It was a pleasure to have the young man sit in my cruiser and tell me the story and see him walk away from an accident that should have claimed his life.

After a thorough investigation, it was determined the young man did everything he could. His choices were limited due to the lack of visibility. Even if he had swerved left or right, he still would have struck the trailer.

The driver of the tractor-trailer was in the wrong. He never should have backed the rig across the road with such low visibility, creating a dangerous situation for other motorists.

That was the night that I met the luckiest kid ever.

Just another quiet evening on patrol.

From Sleepiness to Sheer Terror

It was the summer of 1983 — I was putting in my usual 80 hours a week for the Maine State Police, plus building a home in Unity and helping my wife, Mary, run a dairy bar at the entrance to our driveway.

It seemed like I was on screech for about 22 hours a day, catching a few winks each early morning.

The federal government was telling the state of Maine that troopers could no longer be on duty 24 hours a day and our department was transitioning to shift work, which meant the clock told us when to work and when to go home.

I fought it hard, pretty much ignoring the hourly thing. I made sure I was available for my assigned shift and kept working when I felt I was needed.

I had made friends with part-time Waldo County deputy Rod Sienkiewicz. More than 20 years my senior, he loved law enforcement and often rode with me. We found ourselves in all types of messes just about every time we patrolled together. I could always count on Rod to be of assistance with whatever we tackled. I enjoyed his company and hearing about his family and how important they were to him.

Before I start this story, I need to set the stage. My cruiser was a 1982 Chevrolet Malibu. It was, without a doubt, the worst cruiser I ever had in my career. It was dependable but it was too small, cramped, had no air conditioning and the rear windows wouldn't go down so air didn't circulate in the car. It was hot and uncomfortable and too light for high-speed driving. To put it mildly, I hated this cruiser.

One weekend night, I picked up Rod at his home in Freedom and we headed out on patrol. I told Rod I was extremely tired, as I had gotten home from work at daybreak, grabbed a couple hours of sleep, then toiled on the new home construction all day. I was beat!

We made our way to the Montville/Liberty area to work the 10-4 Diner traffic. It seemed quiet—there wasn't much activity and the police radio was quiet too, so quiet it was getting difficult to keep my eyes open.

My eyes were stinging. I found myself nodding off and my head drooping while I was driving. Rod noticed my condition and more than likely was getting concerned for his safety.

I asked him a huge favor, something I had never done before and never did again. "Rod, would you mind driving? I can't keep my eyes open and I feel like I'm going to fall asleep at any moment."

"Oh, sure Mark, I'd love to," he said, probably with a big sigh of relief that I was willing to get out from behind the wheel.

"OK, but we have to set some guidelines. I just need to close my eyes for 30 minutes so I can stay awake for the rest of the night. If you find someone who needs to be stopped, you tell me and I will make the approach after you stop them. If someone fails to stop for you, pull over and I will take the wheel. If HQ calls on the radio, let me know," I told him.

"Sure, sure Mark, we can do that."

With that, I pulled over and let Rod drive my cruiser. I thought all I needed was to shut my eyes for a few minutes and everything would be fine. I don't think I had even plunked on the passenger side before I was out like a light.

I don't know how long I had been snoozing when I awoke to Rod shaking my shoulder. "Mark, Mark! There's been a shooting and they're chasing the guy right now and they're coming our way," Rod screamed.

I awoke with a shudder and was utterly confused. "What? What?" I hollered back at Rod. He repeated it and finally after coming to, I told Rod to pull over.

Once behind the wheel, I got more facts from HQ. Apparently, a jealous husband had gone to a dance club in Waterville, caught his wife dancing with another man, pulled out a gun and shot them both on the dance floor.

The husband fled the club with local police and troopers in pursuit. They had gone north into Fairfield, across the three bridges and headed east. That meant, more than likely, the shooter would be driving directly into my patrol area.

Those people who know the area and the roads between Montville and Benton know they are narrow, winding and very hilly with lots of quick dips and knolls—the kind of knolls called "Yesmaams." They put your stomach up into your throat. The roads also go from paved to dirt and back to paved.

Even though seatbelt use was not a law in 1983, this was a case where seatbelts were mandatory for our safety. Plus, it would be the only thing that would keep me in my seat as I raced toward the shooter.

I immediately drove toward the chase that was headed toward us. If you have ever been to Disney World on an E-Ride, you have some idea what it was like.

Rod and I had about 20 miles to go over back roads. I don't think the tires touched the pavement very often but the bottom of the cruiser sure did ... and sparks flew everywhere. We must have looked like a crashing rocket. Rod hung on for dear life as we made our way there, and he encouraged me to go faster.

I listened to the radio for updates on the chase and made adjustments so I would, hopefully, come out in front of it.

In Albion, we headed across the Benton Road. Finally, the suspect drove onto a woods road and ran into the woods. Police were right on his tail. When we made it to the scene, the suspect had just been captured and was being led out of the woods.

After that wild ride, I thought the least I could do was to get out and open the rear door of their cruiser so they could place the murder suspect in it. We cleared the scene and headed back toward our patrol area. One thing for sure though, I don't remember being one bit tired for the rest of that night.

Just another day in the life.

"Looking for Something to Drink"

Sometimes things just fell into place and a crime was quickly solved. Open and shut. It didn't happen all that often, but when it did, it was memorable.

One thing I liked about winter was that the snow could be quite helpful either proving or disproving something at a potential crime scene. And if the snow was fresh, it was very easy to track a person or vehicle.

This story is about tracking burglars through the snow.

One cold winter day I got a call from a Unity resident who owned a camp on Unity Pond. The caller said an alarm had gone off at his year-round residence, advising him that someone had entered his camp on the lake.

The majority of alarm calls were false, but we had to make sure each time there was no problem.

This man had rigged a system so that if someone stepped on a mat inside his camp, an alarm rang inside his home.

I asked him if a squirrel could set it off and he replied, "Only if it weighs more than 50 pounds."

Having not seen many 50-pound squirrels in my life, I thought it would be a good idea to check it out.

I was not able to drive all the way to the camp that winter, so I parked my cruiser and hiked in. It was less than a quarter-mile trek, and if someone was still inside the camp, I would have the element of surprise on my side.

I didn't notice any footprints on the camp road so very quietly, I looked in the windows as I made my way around the cottage to the lakeside.

Sure enough, footprints led from the lake to the front door of the camp. I couldn't see anyone inside and so I more carefully checked the footprints. It appeared that whoever had broken into the camp had made their way back from whence they came.

The front door had been kicked in and most of the cupboards had been gone through and cabinet doors were left ajar. There wasn't a lot of damage, except for the front door, but obviously the people who broke in had been looking for something.

Not finding anyone hiding inside the camp, I started tracking the suspect across the lake.

It became obvious the tracks had been made by two people. They seemed to be heading right for an ice fishing shack on the lake.

I kept telling myself this was too easy.

No way would I find someone still in that shack. But sure enough, the tracks went right up to and inside the hut.

I listened for a while to see what I could hear—two young men laughed and giggled about nothing. I let them be for a while hoping they would say something about breaking into the camp. Not a word was uttered about that, however.

Not being too patient, I thought it was about time they knew I was there. I put my hand on the door handle and, without warning, I quickly yanked the door open. I thought both of them were going to jump through the roof; I scared the living daylights out of them.

Plus, one of them was putting a bottle of booze to his lips and that landed on the floor as he jumped and screamed.

"What are you boys doing," I asked.

"Nothing! Nothing," they both exclaimed.

"You old enough to drink?"

"No."

"So where did you get that booze," I asked.

"What booze?"

"OK, boys, let's start over. And this time try telling me the truth cause I know exactly what you have done," I told them.

They attempted once more to deny their deed, but after a little more lecturing from me they fessed up to breaking into the camp and stealing the booze.

"We just wanted something to drink," they said.

The boys were rounded up, turned over to their parents and charged with burglary and theft.

I wish all cases went that smoothly.

Just another quiet day in the life.

Trooper Shot Chasing Escapees

I love going into the archives and looking up old Maine State Police cases. I found this one in one of my dad's notebooks when he went through the State Police Academy in 1954. The following incident occurred the afternoon of March 21, 1946, in Kittery and York.

A few days prior, 17 youths had escaped from the South Windham men's reformatory. Trooper Royal Spofford, a former standout high school and college athlete, was shot in the neck while pursuing the escapees.

I found a newspaper account of unknown origin of the incident while reading the case file from the notebooks my father kept. The file also contained Trooper Spofford's statement, along with a statement from one of the escapees.

It sure is interesting reading:

"Recaptured after a gun battle in York and Kittery yesterday afternoon, in which a Maine State Trooper was wounded, five of the 17 youths who escaped from South Windham men's reformatory will face arraignment in York...before Trial Justice Lester M. Bragdon.

"The escapees were held overnight in York County Jail at Alfred.

"Four others of the 17 who escaped were recaptured in a search that stretched from the Canadian border to Fall River, Massachusetts. Eight others still are at large.

"The quintet fought a running gun battle with Trooper Royal Spofford on U.S. Highway 1 and on South Road, York.

"Trooper Spofford, a former Kennebunk High School and University of Maine athlete, saw a beach wagon going north from the Kittery traffic circle which bore a registration number closely resembling one that had been reported stolen. He gave chase and coming abreast of the beach wagon, ordered the driver to pull over.

"Instead of obeying his order, one of the occupants opened fire at point-blank range, the first shot wounding the trooper in the neck.

"Putting on speed, the beach wagon pulled away with the wounded Spofford in pursuit. Traveling at speeds up to 75 miles an hour, the jail breakers continued to fire at the trooper, one shot striking his left front fender.

Three leave car

"The jail breakers turned right at Rice's Hill, York, going down the South Road. Near Sewell's Bridge, they stopped and three men jumped out, making a break for the woods; two continued on with the beach wagon.

"Jumping from his cruiser, Spofford fired over the head of one of the youths, Herbert Perkins, 19, of Belfast, who had been serving a sentence for breaking, entering and larceny. He dropped to the ground. While Perkins was walking back to surrender, Woodrow Bowden, a discharged veteran living in the neighborhood, had discovered Charles McGilvray, 17, of Portland, a juvenile delinquent, hiding behind a tree and pointed him out to Spofford.

"Trooper Spofford put the boys in his cruiser and, despite his wounds, drove them to the York Jail.

"Upon Spofford's arrival at the jail, Fire Chief William Sullivan, who had just returned from a grass fire on Sewell's Hill, drove him to the York hospital where his wound was treated. Spofford's condition was reported as good.

Cox sights two youths

"In the meantime, Myron Cox, special policeman and fireman of York, returning from the fire on Sewell's Hill, saw a speeding beach wagon, with the rear door flying open, turn into Harbor Lights, an estate owned by J.W. Bowman of New York. Two boys, Mayland Pushard, 19, of Gardiner, who was under sentence for assault and battery, and Roland Levesque, 17, of Portland, incorrigible, jumped out when they found a chain across the driveway and disappeared on the grounds of the estate.

"Mr. Cox, becoming suspicious, halted the first passing car, asking the driver to call the police. Mr. Sullivan, who also is acting police chief, already was on his way to the scene after leaving Trooper Spofford at the hospital. Shortly after, Mr. Cox saw Carl Geisinger, 19, of Portland, who was serving a sentence for breaking, entering and larceny, escaping through the fields.

"Mr. Bowden, who had returned to his home for a gun, was coming up the road, spotted Geisinger and called to Cox to hold him. Geisinger surrendered at gunpoint to Cox.

"Levesque and Pushard were captured an hour later near the Bowman place by a posse of state police and civilians.

Plane aids hunt

"While the posse scoured the York River marshes for Levesque and Pushard, two Portsmouth flyers, Phil Davis and James "Casey" Massacek, searched the ground from the air for more than an hour.

"Police recovered the weapons, a 38.55-caliber rifle, a .22-caliber rifle, and a 10-gauge shotgun, which had been stolen from Carl Garten of Blackstrap Road, Falmouth.

"The boys told police they had stolen the beach wagon in Westbrook, and had been to Boston and Lynn, Mass. While in Lynn, they left one of their group, believed by police to be Richard Madden, 18, formerly of Lynn and Fall River, Mass.

"The five men, who were questioned by Maine State Police Lt. Robert Marx, were among the 17 inmates of the South Windham reformatory who made a break from that institution Wednesday night. Of the 17 who escaped, nine have been recaptured."

Just another day in the life of a trooper, way back when.

Scurrying Rats

It was a nice, warm, summer evening when I got a call from a law enforcement friend who asked to ride along with me for the night.

I enjoyed ride-alongs. They were company, an extra set of eyes and ears, and made the night go by much quicker. The department encouraged ride-alongs for people interested in being troopers; it provided them with firsthand knowledge of what it was like in the real world.

The only problem was that I had to go to Skowhegan to pick him up. It was a ways outside of my patrol area, and sometimes it was hard to get away. But I committed to it and made a mad dash to get him and get back to my zone as quickly as possible.

The other situation was that I could come across an incident requiring law enforcement assistance while traveling outside of my assigned area and get tied up. Of course, this is exactly what happened on this particular night.

It was the summer of 1996, and my cruiser was a bright red Camaro sports car with a huge Corvette engine. To say I enjoyed this cruiser is a slight understatement. I had to pinch myself every moment I drove it so I didn't think it was a dream. It was also a great public relations tool that I used at every opportunity.

I had picked up the ride-along and was heading back across Route 2 from Skowhegan to get back to my patrol area. Going by a store in Canaan, my attention went to a vehicle approaching me on the highway. After we passed the store, my ride-along said he thought a fight was taking place in the store's parking lot. I obviously had missed it.

"Are you sure?" I inquired.

"I'm pretty sure."

"Well, let's go check it out."

I flipped the cruiser around on Route 2 and headed back to the store a few hundred yards away. In the parking lot, four men surrounded one man lying on the ground. The four men were in different stages of assaulting the man. One was bent over the victim's head and pummeling him with his fists. The other three were kicking at him. The man was curled up as best as he could in the fetal position to protect himself. And then there were the onlookers. It became quite clear it was a group thing and these guys were after the one man.

How could I tell this? Easy. The people pelting the victim were part of an outlaw motorcycle gang delivering their brand of justice.

I slammed on the brakes and came to a screeching halt within feet of the scuffle in the parking lot. These guys must have been quite surprised when a bright red sports car came out of nowhere and landed beside them.

I jumped out of the cruiser, ran to the so-called fight, grabbed the man bent over the defenseless victim and stood him up. He was still swinging until he saw that a trooper was holding him up.

He abruptly stopped and his eyes widened. All the bystanders quickly retreated to their cars and motorcycles. They looked like scurrying rats trying to find the nearest hole in which to crawl. Cars and bikes started up all over the place and took off like rockets. I honestly felt like Batman coming to the rescue of a poor victim.

I still had a hold of the coward who had ganged up on the victim with three others. The victim quickly got to his feet, and I recognized him immediately. He recognized me as well and very excitedly hollered, "Am I glad to see you, Mark!"

"I bet you are," I told him.

I knew the underlying problem with the outlaw motorcycle group. The members were ticked because the victim and some others had started their own motorcycle group, using part of the outlaw motorcycle gang's logo for their logo.

This apparently did not set well with the outlaw members, and they were willing to commit criminal acts to protect the logo.

I had the swinger by the nape of his neck and asked the victim, "What do you want to do with this guy? You want him arrested and taken to jail? You want to press charges?"

My victim thought for a minute and finally said, "No, let him go. I'll deal with this another way."

"Are you sure about that?" I protested.

"Yep, let him go."

When I released him, I never saw a man scurry off as quickly as he did. All the rest of his group had taken off and left him behind without a ride. He ran off on foot down the road to get away, finally disappearing in the dark.

I made sure the victim didn't need medical attention and that he could get to wherever he needed to go. Once he was taken care of, I started off for my patrol area, shaking my head wondering why in the world he wouldn't press charges. But he didn't. Until later that is.

Just another day in the life of a trooper.

My Canadian Trip

How times have changed.

Just before I retired I was notified that a trooper who patrols Down East got in trouble for chasing a driver suspected of operating under the influence from Maine into Canada.

A friend told me a story in the Bangor Daily News detailed the facts of the case. Reading it reminded me of a trip I had made many years ago to our friendly neighbor to the north.

One day, I got a call from our then-colonel. It was in the very early '80s, when I patrolled the northern portion of Piscataquis and Somerset counties.

Whenever a trooper gets a call from the colonel that he wants to meet in his office, it can't be good news. I thought for sure I had done something wrong and was about to be reprimanded.

Still expecting the worst, I met the colonel in his office and he told me that he had a little chore for me to do.

"I need you to go over to the Legislature and meet with the Senate president and House speaker. They have a problem, and I believe you can take care of it for them," he said.

"OK" was about all I could muster at the time, being rather relieved to learn that I was not in hot water.

For me, though, going to the Legislature was like going to the moon.

It was completely foreign; I did not know my way around. Plus, I did not like hanging out or being around politicians. I really enjoyed just working and staying up in the north country where no one bothered me, and I could pretty much stay by myself.

But since the colonel had assigned me the chore, I wandered over to the Legislature and met with the two gentlemen who had requested to see a trooper from the north country.

It seemed that one of them operated some sporting camps in Piscataquis County. A Canadian outfit had rented several of the cabins for a lengthy spell, and when the campers all left town, a check had been written to cover the bill.

The problem was that the check had bounced higher than a superball. The legislator was stuck with several thousands of dollars being owed to him. The Canadian camper apparently felt quite comfortable staying on his side of the border and refusing to make the check good.

I was supplied with copies of the rubbery checks and was asked if I could do anything about it.

"You realize it is Canada, right," I sarcastically mentioned.

"Yes, I do, but can you do what you can with it and see what happens?" the sporting camps owner/legislator replied.

"I'll see what I can for you," was about all I could muster up before leaving the Capitol building and heading north to where I feel much more comfortable.

Leaving the Augusta area armed with some bad checks and seemingly the permission of the people who most mattered, I figured I had carte blanche to do what was necessary to bring the rubber-check writers to justice.

Never mind the matter of the international border.

I promptly drove to Greenville and started working on the case. As a courtesy to the Royal Canadian Mounted Police, I let them know what I was about to do. They were extremely helpful, advising me they were well aware of this particular company — including what it was and where it was located.

After gathering the information, I jumped in my cruiser and headed for the city of Saint-Georges, Quebec, crossing the border above Jackman. I remember the funny looks I received passing through Canadian customs, but I told them I was on official business, which got me right through without any holdups.

Upon arriving in the city of Saint-Georges, I drove to the place of business and entered the building. A secretary met me, and I told her that I needed to see the owner of the company.

"May I say who is calling on him?" she asked.

"Tell him the Maine State Police are here to see him," I said.

I don't think the door had even closed behind her before it swung open again, and the owner came right out and invited me in his office.

"What can I do for you, Sir?" he asked.

I opened a folder and placed all of the bad checks on his desk.

"We have a problem. You owe this person all this money, and you are apparently ignoring him. Where I come from, you can't write a check without having money in the bank to back it up. If you do, then you go to jail. When I return to Maine today, I am either going to have this amount of money with me, or I am going to have you with me. And I don't take checks."

Of course I was bluffing, but it seemed to work. He quickly gave me the amount he owed in U.S. currency.

"Is this the last I see of you?" he asked.

"As long as you don't write any more bad checks," I replied.

With that, I left his business, thanked the Royal Canadian Mounted Police who assisted me and headed back to the great state of Maine. And I didn't get in any trouble for crossing the border.

How times have changed.

Just another day in the life.

Paranoia

I used to find it interesting that just the presence of a uniformed trooper or a cruiser at inopportune times caused strange reactions. The reactions weren't necessarily intentional, sometimes they just happened. It's sort of like parking an unmanned Maine State Police cruiser in a crossover on the interstate. Once a driver, myself included, sees the cruiser, s/he automatically steps on the brake. The cruiser produces the desired effect of slowing traffic, if even for a short distance or time.

Here are a couple of instances where by just showing up I unintentionally elicited reactions without initially knowing what was going on. After the fact, I thought the situations were kind of humorous.

One night on patrol, a fellow named Fred was riding with me. It was a time when most stores were not open all night, but there was one just outside of Augusta where we could grab a snack.

When we approached the store on Route 202, I observed an SUV-type of vehicle pull into the store from the opposite direction. We were still a distance away and when I turned into the store parking lot, most of the occupants had gotten out of the vehicle.

As I watched them walk into the store, it was obvious they all had been drinking; some were quite intoxicated. I did not see who had been behind the wheel and I surely couldn't charge them all with operating under the influence.

So I thought I would wait them out as I knew they had to leave at some point. I did my best not to show any interest in their activities so they would eventually leave. But the cruiser stuck out way too much not to be noticed.

One by one, the occupants of the vehicle came out of the store with a fresh supply of alcohol. Each one re-entered the vehicle. Finally, everyone who had exited the vehicle had returned. The interesting thing was, no one got behind the wheel. Everyone just sat in the vehicle; no one took the responsibility of being the operator. We all sat and waited and none of us made a move. I wondered just how long the waiting game was going to last.

After close to 20 minutes or so and after Fred and I had a good laugh, I walked to the vehicle. They were a good bunch of guys who were having a bachelor party and they had run out of spirits. Rather than have one person go get the beer, they all decided to go for the ride. Once in the parking lot they saw the cruiser and no one wanted to get into trouble so no one got back in the driver's seat. They were laughing as hard as Fred and I did. The vehicle was like a headless horseman.

We made arrangements for another friend to get them and drive them safely back to the party. Thinking about that vehicle full of guys with no driver always makes me chuckle.

Another time while on duty, I ran into a longtime friend in Fairfield. Lindsay was in the construction business and told me he was renovating an old camp into a year-round home for a customer on Snow Pond in Oakland. I had a few minutes and wanted to look at it. So Lindsay jumped into my cruiser and off we went to look at the project.

I pulled down the camp road and stopped near the lake right beside the camp, which was lifted up on posts. We walked around the structure as Lindsay explained what had been done and what needed to be done. He explained that the couple who owned it were living in it as construction progressed.

We were standing just outside the posts and could hear the second-floor toilet flushing over and over. The pump was running to supply the toilet. Lindsay thought something might be wrong, as he didn't think anyone should be inside during the day. We could not see any water leaks so Lindsay assumed the water was probably just running through the toilet. He said he would notify the owner.

We hung around for about 20 minutes or so checking things over then left. I dropped Lindsay off in Fairfield and went on my way. It wasn't too long after dropping him off that Lindsay, laughing uncontrollably, called me on my cell phone.

"What's up anyway?" I asked.

"You would not believe what was going on when we were at the camp," he said.

"I'll bite. What did we miss?"

"Well, when we pulled into the yard, the owner's girlfriend saw the cruiser and panicked. She thought you were going to raid the house. So she gathered up all the marijuana they had and started flushing it down the toilet, and flushed until it was all gone. Then she told her boyfriend, 'There will be no more dope in the house from this point forward!' So that explains the water running while we were there."

We both got a big chuckle and I realized that the mere presence of a cruiser or person in uniform can sometimes cause quite a stir.

Just another day in the life.

By The Book

Professional police officers have a set of standards by which they live and work.

The Maine State Police had several policy books that were our bibles. As long as we followed the policies and procedures, we knew, in the end, there would not be a problem.

It was how we built trust with the public we worked for. In addition, the policies reflect the Maine State Police core values of integrity, fairness, compassion and excellence.

Criminals, though, do not follow such rules.

So it was up to us, the good guys, to figure out ways to get the bad guys and stay within the law. Countless times, while investigating major crimes, it was tempting to cross that line to get the information needed to make arrests.

But for me, I couldn't do it. I know it's a long road without a curve and sooner or later, I knew my suspect would mess up and I would be there to pick up the pieces.

This story is an example of needing more information before I could make an arrest. It was frustrating to be so close but still to need more. Knowing and proving are two different things.

As with a lot of cases, good information comes when two people fight. One of them always wants to hurt the other one to get back at them. This particular case started in 1984 with a phone call.

"Hey Mark, do you know Fred Harris up there in Troy?"

"Yes I do. He's that farmer, right?"

"Yep. Well he's got a stolen truck parked out on his property. It was almost new when he got it and it's been there for a long time. He won't register it cause it's stolen but he's taken most of the good stuff off it and put it on his other trucks," I was told.

"Really?!"

"Yep, it's a big red commercial truck. And I want you to catch him with it."

"Well, I need more than you just telling me it's stolen," I told the informer.

"All I know is it came from out of state and he's had it for about five years."

"Well thanks a lot, I'll see what I can do," I advised the caller.

This was the frustrating part of law enforcement. The caller was a trusting, solid informer. But this person claiming the truck was stolen was not enough for me to grab it. I had to prove it was stolen before taking any legal action. There were several ways to do this, including interviewing the suspect. Sometimes that works and sometimes it doesn't.

What I needed was to get the vehicle identification number (VIN) to see whether, in fact, it was stolen. It was so much easier doing an interview when I already knew the facts.

I had a friend in the Maine State Police who was so secretive that most people didn't know what he did or when he was around. His work was phenomenal. Whenever I needed something done of a secret nature, I called on him to do it. He never let me down and always provided me with the pertinent information.

He also was part of the first unit to work strictly with stolen vehicles.

I gave him a call and told him what I needed, and we agreed to meet late one night the following week. It was well after midnight when we hooked up. I took him to the farm and told him the truck in question was somewhere on the farm behind a barn.

My friend took off under the cover of darkness. Our rendezvous point was up the road in about a half-hour. I quietly drove along the road without headlights and waited in the darkness for the trooper to return.

He made it back to my cruiser, but I wasn't so sure I was going to let him back in. He smelled a lot like the animals on the farm and I didn't want that smell permeating my cruiser. He laughed about running smack dab into one of the cows, and how it had scared the cow as much as it had scared him.

Lo and behold, my friend had the information that I needed to prove whether this vehicle was, in fact, stolen. So, reluctantly, I let him back in the cruiser. I went home and called Maine State Police Headquarters. They ran the VIN through the computers and sure enough, the truck was stolen from out of state in the late '70s.

I had what I needed. My next step would be to approach the farmer. With the information I had he would know that I knew he was in possession of a stolen vehicle.

The first chance I got I went looking for ol' Fred. When I drove into his dooryard, he greeted me in the same fashion he always did, with a friendly welcome. I told him that this time I was there for a serious reason. His smile turned to a frown and he asked what the problem was.

"Well Fred, why don't you tell me about that stolen truck you have out behind the barn."

He hung his head and his shoulders drooped. It was almost as if he was relieved. "You have no idea what that truck has put me through all these years. I'm glad you know about it now," he said.

"Why don't you tell me the whole story, Fred, from the beginning to right now," I suggested.

"Well, I was at an agriculture fair out of state and one evening I attended a little party after the fair shut down. I was talking with this guy that was there and we got to talking about trucks and so forth. You know I always drove around in trucks that were worn out, Mark. So I told this guy, who I have no idea who he is, I told him how I would love to get a newer truck sometime, but I just don't have that kind of money. He asked me if I had $500 with me and I told him I did. He told me that he knew a guy that wanted to get rid of a truck and would take $500 for it. I told him sure. So the guy leaves and told me to stay put, he would be right back with the truck.

"Sure enough, not a half-hour passed and the guy returns to the party and gets me to come and look at the truck. He told me, 'Here you go — $500.' Mark, the paint on the door wasn't even dry where they covered over the name of the business they stole it from. All I kept saying to myself was, 'Uh-oh, I'm in trouble.'

"I didn't want to seem like a big baby so I took the truck and immediately drove it home, sweating all the way, scared to death that I was going to get caught with this truck. I got it home and it never left the property since I got it here. I have fretted over this thing for years. I am relieved that you found out and I can get it over with," he said.

I ended up confiscating the truck from Fred the farmer. The insurance company was notified of the recovery, and a person from the company came and got it and recovered some of the money that had been paid on it years earlier.

I let Fred sweat it out a while longer but, in the end, I never charged him with the crime. I almost think, looking at the big picture, that he was a victim in the case.

Just another day in the life of a trooper.

Skipping School

You know that first lovely spring day after a long, cold winter? The warmth of the sun, the smell of spring in the light breeze, the sounds of birds arriving from their winter vacation? This particular day, in May 1980, was one such day.

Everyone, students included, wanted to be outside enjoying the weather and escaping the everyday doldrums of the previous several months.

Three particular students, however, were headed straight for trouble on this day. School was not on their list of things to do for the day.

One student, driving his little Chevette, picked up two friends, a male and a female. Rather than go to school like they usually did they headed back home to get daddy's booze. Soon they were back in the Chevette and headed for big trouble. With alcohol courage, they started to terrorize the highways in the quiet Somerset County towns around Embden and Solon.

It wasn't long before they caught the attention of a trooper, who gave chase but lost them. Once the chase was called in, other area troopers took note and worked their way in that direction. I was no exception. I was in Abbott late that morning, 25 miles from Route 201 in Bingham, just north of the fray.

Never knowing what direction a chase might turn and not knowing how things might turn out, I headed that way.

Then a call came in to Maine State Police Headquarters about a small blue vehicle with three kids in it that had left the roadway, gone across a lawn, and almost run over an elderly gentleman raking his lawn.

The gentleman sought refuge on his front porch as the kids spun up his lawn, whooping and hollering as they did so. Obviously, these were the same teens who had just eluded a trooper.

Another trooper, Barry Delong, spotted the suspect vehicle and made the traffic stop in North Embden on Route 201A. While Barry approached the Chevette on foot, the driver pulled ahead a bit, drawing Barry farther away from the cruiser. Then the driver threw the vehicle into reverse and attempted to back over Barry.

The suspects took off at a high rate of speed, once again trying to avoid capture. These kids had upped the ante considerably by nearly running over an innocent gentleman and attempting to injure a trooper. Delong was not going to let them kill someone or themselves.

Barry, an excellent driver, pursued them north onto Route 201. Hearing this on the radio, I picked up my speed across Route 16 heading toward Bingham. My goal was to get south of Bingham and set up a roadblock.

There was a slight problem, though. Route 16 was full of frost heaves and potholes. It was a winding, older secondary road anyway, and the frost had rendered it nearly impassable.

Most of the time my cruiser was airborne; I flew over knolls, bottomed out often and left a trail of sparks. I made it to Bingham in record time, though, as Trooper Delong was still chasing the school-skippers north on Route 201, heading into Bingham.

Delong informed Maine State Police HQ of his progress and the location and the actions of the suspect vehicle. Barry had to make some decisions. The erratic driver would soon be going by a school; Barry was not going to allow that to happen.

As he pulled up alongside the suspect vehicle on a long, straight section of Route 201 just south of Bingham, he motioned for them to pull over. With windows down, they stretched out their arms, giving him the finger and screaming obscenities at him. Good old alcohol courage at work.

Traveling side-by-side at 90 mph along Route 201, the kids had one more trick up their proverbial sleeves. The driver rammed the side of the Barry's cruiser, putting both vehicles on two wheels.

That's when Barry put an end to the chase; he rammed the suspect vehicle, causing it to go out of control. As Barry pulled ahead, he saw a horrifying sight in his rear view mirror. The suspect vehicle flipped end over end, ejecting the driver out of the vehicle. He flew 20 feet into the air and landed in the roadway. Trooper Delong called for an ambulance as he turned to go back to assist the young kids.

I made it to the scene as Barry was turning around in the roadway. I assisted with the injured and made the necessary arrests. Fortunately, the young man survived the ordeal with only an arm injury.

The vehicles didn't make out so well. The suspect Chevette was totaled and Barry's cruiser had extensive passenger side damage. His sergeant told him to pull out the fender so it wouldn't rub against the tire and go back to work. My cruiser had a sprung frame from all the hard landings traveling over all the roller coaster dips on Route 16.

The ride back to my patrol area was much slower as I finally got to enjoy that beautiful spring day.

Just another day in the life.

Where Did That Stop Sign Come From?

Here's a funny little story that happened to me long ago. It was about 2 a.m. when I slid into Greenville after patrolling the northern parts of Piscataquis and Somerset counties. Usually before going home I swung through town to make sure all was quiet, and to look for Mickey Squiers, a Greenville officer, to see if anything interesting had happened in town that night.

I made my way to the east side of Greenville where the town offices were. It was a routine place for law enforcement to park and observe the major intersection. Most traffic had to go through there, including anyone traveling through town after midnight. So it was a good place to check for drunk drivers.

If we placed our cruisers just right, they weren't visible from the roadway so it was a favorite spot to park and converse while watching the comings and goings.

After finding the town quiet, I slowly drove by the lot, straining to see if Mickey was tucked in the hiding spot. I spotted the Greenville cruiser and pulled in to talk with Mickey.

But I was not paying proper attention to the roadway. There was absolutely no traffic, but I wasn't where I thought I was. I quickly turned the wheel to pull in, all the while keeping an eye on the Greenville cruiser and not on the road.

"Clang!"

Since I am a jumpy person, and it was in the middle of the night, this was quite a surprise. I turned every which way to see what in the world had made the noise. I was stumped.

Apparently, the noise had jolted Mickey awake. He was parked a good 50 yards away and had nodded off in his cruiser.

Not seeing any danger signs, I continued driving into the parking lot. It was then that the telltale sign of what had happened became apparent. Something was scraping underneath the cruiser. I had run smack-dab into the stop sign at the end of the street and flattened it under my cruiser. I pulled up alongside Mickey, who was laughing almost hysterically.

"What are you doing, you numbskull?" he asked.

"I can't believe I just ran over that sign. I am reporting it to you so you can let the public works people know to stand it back up," I told him. "I'm just glad it's in the middle of the night under the cover of darkness, so no one saw that Keystone Kop move!"

I checked the front of my cruiser and there wasn't a scratch. That was good, as I would have had to report it to my supervisor. So all that had to be done was to stand up the flattened stop sign.

Right next door to the parking lot entrance was a service station and the manager of the business lived upstairs. Because it was a busy part of town, this particular person had been asked several times over the years if he had ever witnessed any of the crimes that had occurred around his establishment.

Every time, without fail, he responded that he "never saw or heard anything." It was almost a joke, as even before officers asked him the question, we knew the response would be, "Nope, never heard or saw a thing."

The very next day, while Mickey was in his office, that particular person came in to report that the previous night he saw a state police cruiser run over the stop sign at the end of the street. And he believed the trooper was that Nickerson fellow.

I will never forget what Mickey told him. "You son of a gun. You never see one stinking thing happen when I'm looking for a bad guy, but Nickerson hits a stop sign and you come running over to turn him in? Get out of my office!"

Except for some hurt pride, that was the end of that.

Just another day in the life.

So, Sue Me!

One thing I never thought about when applying for, going through the hiring process and finally becoming a Maine State Police trooper, was getting sued.

Even though we had training on the issue at the Maine State Police Academy, I didn't think it would happen to me as long as I did the job with good intentions and as the law allowed.

However, more than a few times during the course of my career, I found myself sitting on the hot seat. No lawsuit, though, ever went to trial or was settled for a monetary gain on behalf of the defendant. But there was one case when a defendant got special treatment. Let me tell you about this little adventure.

Of course, most of the time when I found myself in some type of pickle, my friend and cohort, Game Warden John Ford, was usually the instigator. Such was the case in this case.

But not every instance, like the time when a fellow had a two-by-four cocked like he was Babe Ruth ready to smack me over the head. John launched into campaign mode and shook the man's hand, and asked for his vote when he ran for sheriff.

Or the time when we changed our names (John Boy became chief of the Maine State Police, Allan Weeks, while I became Bob Keating, then-chief of the Belfast Police Department) to escape from a couple of misguided elderly ladies who thought we were derelict in performing our duties. That was a close one.

This particular time, while minding my own business and doing routine patrol work, I ran into John Boy.

"Nicky, ol' boy." This is actually a cleaned-up version of how he used to, and still does, greet me. "I need a little favor."

That's when I should have run the other way as fast as my legs would carry me.

"Now what have you done?" I nervously asked.

"I got this case over in Thorndike. This guy bought a Maine resident hunting license but he isn't a Maine resident. He's from Connecticut and he has a Connecticut driver's license. He lives and works there during the week, then each weekend he comes here to his other residence in Thorndike. Now, the law is you must have residency in Maine, have a Maine driver's license and vote in Maine to meet the requirements of being a Maine resident," John explained.

"So what's the problem?"

"Well, I charged him with obtaining a Maine hunting license under false pretenses. Now he wants a trial. But I have to tell you, the clerk in that town is the sweetest little 90-year-old lady and there is no way I am going to make her go to court and testify in any case like this. So I had the case dismissed but warned the suspect that he is not allowed to do what he did again. But he is claiming that he is a Maine resident and I can tell you right now he does not have a Maine driver's license," John Boy said.

"So what do you want me to do?" I asked, already knowing the answer.

"I want you to hunt him down and give him a summons for operating a motor vehicle without a license."

Which is exactly what I did.

We'll call the suspect Mr. C.

Mr. C was not happy about getting a summons. He explained to me that he had to keep his Connecticut license for work due to being a member of a union.

I told Mr. C that he needed to pick one state for his residence — that he couldn't enjoy the benefits of being a resident of both. That was not how it worked. If he was a resident of Connecticut he had to pay for a nonresident hunting license here in Maine. Apparently, Mr. C was rather frugal. Or perhaps cheap.

In those days, court paperwork was rather loose. When I issued the summons, I did it like usual and put "operating w/o license."

The case made its way to Waldo County Superior Court and just as we were all being seated in front of the judge, he read the summons and dismissed the case for lack of wording on the summons.

It was thrown out before it even got started.

Mr. C. and his attorney were rather pleased. The district attorney and I were not, as the issue still loomed in front of us.

I looked at the DA with complete confusion. "What was that?"

He said that the judge had erred and should not have dumped the case.

"So what do I do about it?" I asked.

"Go pinch Mr. C again and this time write on the summons: 'Operating a motor vehicle without a license.' And we'll be right back here in court with it again."

I walked over to Mr. C in front of his attorney and warned him that nothing was settled and the issue remained. I warned him if I saw him driving I would have no choice but to charge him again with the offense.

Before Mr. C could answer, his attorney, a man from Belfast, piped in, pointed his finger at me and said, "If you stop my client, you're going to get sued!"

"So sue me!" I shot right back. I thought I was doing the right thing and enforcing a law. I thought Mr. C was trying to jump through a loophole.

I kept my word and within days I again caught Mr. C driving and issued him another summons.

The local Belfast attorney kept his word, as well, and promptly sued me.

The outcome? Mr. C was probably the first and only person in the state of Maine allowed to have a Maine driver's license and a Connecticut driver's license. Once the agreement was reached, the lawsuit against me was dismissed.

Thanks, John Boy!

Just another day in the life of a trooper.

The Nissen Bread Man

I became friends with a woman in Troy in the early '80s and our friendship continues to this day, even though she has moved away and is a flight attendant for an international commercial airline.

When this particular incident took place and Karen Wales told me her side of the story, all I could do was laugh out loud at the predicament that both of my friends found themselves in, due mostly to their strong personalities and not being afraid to tell it like it is.

During this time, we had a person impersonating a police officer and trying to stop vehicles. When this case went to court, I spoke on behalf of Karen and her concerns.

This, of course, put a slight strain on my friendship with John Ford, but only for a short time. To this day, he still sticks to the action he took that day and I remind him that he was mistaken for the Nissen bread man. The following story was provided to me by Karen, so sit back and enjoy a story from the "victim's" side.

North Dixmont Road is where this story begins. It was in the fall of 1983, some months after moving into our home on the gravel road, which indeed took 25 years to get paved, just as the town clerk had told me it would when I registered my vehicles.

My husband and I had moved to Troy from "away," also known as Maryland. As a side note to this story, my husband was Maine-born, however, I am an Army brat, a daughter of a military family. I never really was from anywhere in particular due to our many moves and new homes.

So it is, that we brats come prepared to live immediately wherever we are. We also have the challenge of not recognizing local personalities.

"The local state trooper will be at the meeting at the firehouse, you going?" asked my neighbor.

The meeting was for the Neighborhood Watch Committee, a title used only for that one-time meeting. There had been some activity on the Bishop Road wherein some bandits had broken into trailers and locals and neighbors thought we needed to discuss a strategy.

It was there that I met Trooper Mark Nickerson. His reputation did not precede him as I had just moved to Troy a few months earlier. I had attended one town meeting in January or February, and got my photo on the front page of the Waterville newspaper, albeit with my name slightly misspelled, a mixed blessing. The photo showed me pointing my finger as I proudly wore my new L.L. Bean vest, a staple clothing item in these parts, and asked about the roads in town.

So it was, at the Neighborhood Watch Committee meeting, that my friendship with Trooper Nickerson began. I asked him about the legality of being able to shoot someone if they refused to leave my property. Feeling uncomfortable with answering directly, he said we could discuss the details another time. I immediately liked his sense of humor and, frankly, thought it was great to know the local state trooper.

Fast forward to the hunting season that fall. With some months under my belt living in Troy, and many miles driven on the North Dixmont Road, my introduction to the Maine Warden

Service began. More importantly, it was my introduction to the power of personality, the man known to all but me, the famous John Ford.

I was driving my Toyota pickup truck toward my home and was about two miles away. As I came up behind a dark pickup, with the license plates obscured, I immediately noticed several things: two men, two rifles in the gun rack in the rear window and some pine branches in the truck bed. The truck was being driven slowly, like the men were looking for something. My first thought was a term I had recently learned from locals, that being "damn Massholes" for hunters from Massachusetts who shot deer from their pickups.

Frustrated with the slow speed and the idea of hunters shooting from trucks, I passed on the left and continued on my way. Within moments, the two men were suddenly right behind me, right on my bumper. How creepy and scary.

So I did what my former Maryland law allowed — namely if one feels threatened and can't determine if the vehicle contains a law enforcement officer, one can go to a safe place, such as home or a store. We had many cases of men impersonating officers, and there even was one in Maine that year.

My heart was racing as I drove the speed limit, since there was snow on the road. I saw that, despite the road conditions, they stayed on my bumper. I said out loud, "What kind of idiots are these?"

Then I saw some blue lights flashing in the grill. "Oh, sure, J.C. Whitney auto parts catalog lights! Who are you kidding?"

The chase continued and a siren started sounding. I was within a half-mile of home, and knew my rights. I was going home whether this was some Mayberry R.F.D. police truck or not. I maintained control of the road as well so as not to let these two men pass me or run me off the road. I had no clue who they were. I just knew that I was alone and cheap gimmicks wouldn't make me stop.

I pulled onto my property, right smack in front of my garage with the truck driver in full pursuit. Now, here is the part of the story that Trooper Nickerson and I both remember the most: the arrival of John Ford into my life. If ever there was a Superman in Waldo County, I met him that day.

With speed reserved for Olympic athletes, he was at my vehicle door as I opened it, ready to confront whomever he had chased. I never made it up off my seat before he was standing before me, shouting a barrage of words, including, "Why didn't you stop for me?"

To which I replied, "Who are you?"

John Ford proceeded to tell me that he was a warden and had his lights and siren activated.

"Am I supposed to know who you are?" I asked. "For all I know, you could be the Nissen bread delivery man. They have the same stripe on their pants."

His pants were the first thing I saw while still sitting in my truck during his tirade. Never tell a superhero you don't like his outfit.

The result for me was that he wrote me up for doing 70 mph in a 40-mph zone and more importantly, for not knowing who he was, I received a charge of evading a police officer. I received a crash course that day in many things.

If I had known the reputation of John Ford, I would not have found myself in court facing him again, standing my ground about not recognizing him. I had to plead guilty to the speeding charge to avoid the other charge of eluding a police officer. Case closed.

Personalities are interesting things; they are not who we truly are. Over the years, as our paths crossed, I remembered him for that day. Additionally, I saw his artwork on calendars, his community work and, as a daughter of a former military policeman, I could appreciate his efforts at policing the county.

We did get off to a bad start, but through Trooper Nickerson I was kept informed and had the great delight of personally

210

telling John via phone recently, that I am grateful he overcame his health concerns.

When he handed the phone back, he asked Trooper Nickerson if I was sincere. Of course I was and am. John Ford has been a superhero in many ways, truly so. It was just unfortunate that on that day long ago that I thought he was bringing bread, not breaking bread!

—Karen Wales

Maine State Police Line of Duty Deaths

It is with sadness that I write this last chapter. Many of these troopers were good friends of mine when they were killed. Each one was a tough loss.

My memory goes back to the day that Trooper Black was shot and killed in South Berwick. I remember that day well, like it was yesterday. My dad was the Lieutenant in charge of the Criminal Division of the Maine State Police.

My mom was on summer break from teaching school and was at home.

I was only 9 years old and I was playing in the field across from our home in Vassalboro. I never played in that field.

I started to hear a siren in the distance and the noise kept getting closer and closer. Hearing a siren near our home was a rarity and I stopped what I was doing to watch whatever was coming.

All of a sudden though, it was my dad's cruiser that came into sight. He turned off the highway onto our road almost on two wheels, and tore into our driveway. He wasn't out of the cruiser but for a minute or two, changed his clothes, jumped back into his cruiser and took off again with the siren whaling as he turned south.

I ran into the house excitedly asking Mom, "What's going on?" She then told me that a trooper had been shot and killed and Dad was on his way to help find one of the men who shot him.

I remember being shocked at this news. I remember what big news that was to our state. It had been 36 years since a Maine state trooper had been killed in the line of duty.

Sixteen years later when Tom Merry was killed it was like getting hit in the chest with a baseball bat. I was a trooper and Tom was in my section. I had seen him two days prior to his death. He was having some administration issues with our supervisor and was complaining up a storm. (His reports were late.) I had taken the day off and was spending the night at my parents' home in Vassalboro. Early in the morning, I got a call from Cpl. Paul Davis. Paul told me that ol' Tom got it last night. I asked, "You mean they fired him?"

"No he was killed in a roadblock in Palmyra."

I couldn't even talk. I just put on my uniform and went to work, trying to help out with whatever needed to be done. Tom was a great guy. It was a huge loss to us.

Drew Griffith was also in my section in Troop D. He made a small mistake that cost him his life. He was complimentary and a pleasure to be around. He loved his work and the people he served respected him for the job he did very well.

His widow, Kate Braestrup, took up his after-retirement passion, becoming a minister. She is the chaplain for the Maine Warden Service and has written several books, including the bestselling memoir *Here If You Need Me*. This wonderful book will make you laugh and cry on the same page.

Following is a list and photo of each Maine State Police trooper killed in the line of duty. They all have stories and someday my goal is to tell their stories and the details of how they died. Let's hope we never have to add another name to this list.

Trooper Emery Gooch, 1885-1924

Officer Gooch was killed when he lost control of his motorcycle in Mattawamkeag on Aug. 9, 1924. A month earlier he had joined the State Highway Patrol.

Trooper Fred Foster, 1898-1925

Trooper Foster was killed when his motorcycle struck a horse hauling a load of hay in Belfast on Aug. 30, 1925. He joined the State Highway Patrol in 1924.

Trooper Frank Wing, 1902-1928

Trooper Wing was killed when his motorcycle collided with an oil truck in Millinocket on Aug. 19, 1928. Two months earlier, he had joined the Maine State Police.

Trooper Charles Black, 1936-1964

Trooper Black was shot to death July 9, 1964, outside Maine National Bank in South Berwick during an armed robbery. He joined the department in 1958.

Trooper Thomas Merry, 1952-1980

Trooper Merry was killed July 12, 1980, in Palmyra. He was struck by a car involved in a high-speed chase. Merry parked his cruiser for a roadblock and was attempting to seek safe cover when he was struck by the fleeing car. He joined the Maine State Police in 1977.

Trooper Michael Veilleux, 1962-1986

Trooper Veilleux was killed June 17, 1986, when he lost control of his cruiser and it overturned in Dayton. The previous month he had graduated from the Maine State Police Academy.

Giles Landry, 1952-1989

Detective Landry was shot to death March 31, 1989, while investigating a child abuse complaint in Leeds. The gunman also killed a woman who was talking with Detective Landry. The gunman then killed himself. Landry joined the Maine State Police in 1976 and was promoted to detective in 1988.

Lt. Rene A. Goupil, 1947-1990

Lt. Goupil suffered a fatal heart attack Jan. 23, 1990, while performing his duties as a member of the training staff for the 42nd Training Troop.

Trooper Jeffrey Parola, 1967-1994

Trooper Parola was killed Nov. 13, 1994, when his cruiser crashed in Sidney. He was a member of the Tactical Team and was responding to a domestic violence call. Parola joined the Maine State Police in 1989.

Trooper James (Drew) Griffith, 1961-1996

Trooper Griffith was killed April 15, 1996, when a vehicle in Warren struck Drew's cruiser as he attempted to make a U-turn to pursue a speeding car. Griffith joined the Maine State Police in 1986.

Glenn Strange, 1951-1997

Detective Strange died of heart problems Oct. 17, 1997, days after arresting a violent drunk driver who had kicked and punched him in the chest in the town of Linneus. He joined the Maine State Police in 1994 following a teaching career. He was promoted to detective weeks before his death.

These photos are on display at State Police Headquarters in Augusta.

About the Author

Mark was born and raised in a Maine State Police family. His father, Millard E. Nickerson Jr., was captain of the Bureau of Criminal Investigation and was posthumously awarded the Legendary Trooper Award, the highest award any Maine trooper can obtain. Mark served 28 years with the Maine State Police, retiring in 2005. He wrote a column for *VillageSoup, The Capital Weekly, The Republican Journal* and the *Courier Gazette*. He is the current President of the Maine State Troopers Foundation, the charitable arm of the Trooper's Association, provides protection to children of war-torn countries each summer at the international Seeds of Peace camp in southern Maine, and loves being a father.

Mark also wrote *Blue Lights in the Night* (North Country Press, 2013).

CPSIA information can be obtained at www.ICGtesting.com
Printed in the USA
BVOW08s2337041115

425554BV00002B/2/P